ANIMAL TRAGIC

Popular misconceptions of
wildlife through the centuries

MALCOLM TAIT

ILLUSTRATIONS BY RUPERT DAVIES

THINK
BOOKS

A THINK BOOK

First published in 2006 by

Think Publishing
The Pall Mall Deposit
124-128 Barlby Road, London W10 6BL
www.think-books.com

Illustrations: Rupert Davies
Sub Editor: Rica Dearman
Designers: Lou Millward and Mark Evans

ISBN-10: 1-84525-015-X
ISBN-13: 978-1-84525-015-7

Printed and bound in Italy by Grafica Veneta S.p.A

The publisher and author have made every effort to ensure the accuracy and
currency of the information in *Animal Tragic*. The publisher and author
disclaim any liability, loss, injury or damage incurred as a consequence,
directly or indirectly, of the use and application of the contents of this book.

'Until you can name all
the animals, shut up and
go back to the garden'

BILL HICKS, COMEDIAN

CONTENTS

AN INTRODUCTION OF SORTS

There's an embedded culture of hyperbole in society based on the concept that more really is more. We no longer get headaches, we get migraines; colds are a thing of the past and it's flu that keeps us off work for a day; genius is attributed to pretty well anyone who shows a little imagination in their field.

And anything vaguely sad or unfortunate is a tragedy. A sporting result goes the wrong way: well, the defender made a tragic mistake. A book is published about human misconceptions of wildlife: it's given the title *Animal Tragic*.

Isn't this a bit over the top? Is it really a tragedy for folk to think that swans sing at the end of their lives, or that elephants are afraid of mice, or that lemmings jump off cliffs to control their numbers? Wouldn't Aristotle, who came up with the ultimate definition of 'tragedy', weep with intellectual frustration to find this charged word so carelessly bandied about?

To Aristotle, a tragic hero was 'a person who is neither perfect in virtue and justice, nor one who falls into misfortune through vice and depravity, but rather, one who succumbs through some miscalculation'. The Aristotelian tragic hero ultimately fails not through some unfortunate external circumstance outside his control, but due to an essential internal fault. Even the most powerful, the wisest, the greatest can have within them a 'tragic flaw' that will prove their undoing.

What applies to the individual can apply to the species. Mankind has long thought of itself as the steward of this planet, holding dominion over every creature and plant upon it, and with the power to shape it in any way wished. We think of ourselves as the most powerful species on Earth, its fate lying in our hands and our hands alone.

Yet as this book shows, mankind has a long history of misunderstanding the true nature of the rest of this planet's inhabitants. Even today, there's so much we still struggle to comprehend. Our knowledge of animals is vastly incomplete, yet still we believe we are their masters.

Could this hubris be mankind's own 'tragic flaw'? Could our insistence on superiority over creatures we do not fully understand and which we cannot live without bring about our own downfall? Are we in the process of orchestrating our own tragedy?

This is the reason for the title of this book. It exposes the human arrogance of a craving for power based on a flawed understanding. Not only that, it also rhymes quite nicely with the old British children's programme *Animal Magic*. So I suppose that's two good reasons.

And one final thing. Aristotle may have defined tragedy for generations of future playwrights, thinkers and essayists, but he also thought that swallows hibernated and that robins and redstarts changed into each other.

Ah, well. Even a genius has flaws.

MALCOLM TAIT, MARCH 2006

CHAPTER 1

Everyday errors

In which commonly accepted knowledge about
wildlife is shown to be steeped in inaccuracy

The bat

It has been said that...

Someone who is incapable of sight is 'blind as a bat' because, well, bats are blind.

The truth

There are no species of blind bat that exist in the world and, although a few species do have poor eyesight, many of them can see very well indeed. Fruit bats, in particular, have very good eyesight. The assumption that bats in general cannot see derives from their remarkable facility of echolocation which they use at night when eyesight would be largely redundant. As they do not need their eyesight, then presumably it doesn't work.

In fact most bats can probably see better than humans can at dusk. But it's at night that their echolocation really comes into its own. They emit rapid series of really quite loud ultrasounds across a variety of frequencies, depending on the species, which bounce back off the objects around them, providing a sonar description of their immediate environment. In this way they can tell the difference between, say, a tree and a moth, and catch the latter while avoiding the former.

This remarkable ability also gives the lie to the idea that bats can get caught in your hair. If a creature is able to pick its way during the darkest of nights through heavily wooded areas at speeds of up to 30mph, and catch up to 3,000 midges on its travels, then it's hardly going to have much difficulty dodging your head.

And in a similar vein...

Dracula is just a story and, other than the fact that some feed on blood, there is nothing Dracula-like about bats in the real world, right? Not quite. The saliva of vampire bats contains a glycoprotein that help keeps the source of their meals from coagulating. Proving that scientists can have fun with words just like anyone else, the name of this protein is draculin.

The bee

It has been said that...

The saying 'the bee's knees', which means excellence, is an Italian-American corruption of 'the business', which has the same meaning.

The truth

This term is indeed of US origin, but actually finds its roots in fashionable American slang. In 1921, various possessions of the cat – its miaow, whiskers and pyjamas – were used to express the height of excellence. The 'cat's pyjamas' was probably the first such phrase, based on the thinking that as a cat is a highly elegant creature, its pyjamas (an item of clothing that was by now very fashionable) must be most stylish indeed.

Other phrases soon followed, most of them complete nonsense. Something very fine was variously alluded to as the caterpillar's kimono, the elephant's manicure, the eel's ankle, the canary's tusks or the bullfrog's beard. Very few of these sayings outlasted the flapper years, but 'bee's knees' has kept going right up until the present day.

Perhaps it's because, unlike the other phrases, it has some root in the natural world. Canaries may not have tusks, but bees certainly have knees. The knee is effectively just a joint between the upper and lower segments of an animal's legs, so it's quite acceptable to give this anatomic word to an insect as well as a human, although 'femur-tibial joint' is a more scientifically preferred term.

And on the back of a bee's hind leg, just below the knee, it carries a special sac, which is known as a corbicula, into which it collects its golden yellow pollen as it flies from flower to flower. This package of beauty is clearly visible, and truly looks like 'the bee's knees'.

And in a similar vein...
The dreaded Africanised honey bee is believed by
many to be more toxic than the European honey bee,
but in fact its sting is marginally less poisonous. The
danger lies in the sheer quantity of stings, as the bee,
only a recent hybridisation and therefore less used to
human interference, defends itself in huge numbers.

The cranefly

It has been said that...

The cranefly is a poison-carrying insect.

The truth

Craneflies – often known as Daddy long-legs in Britain because of their disproportionately large limbs – are familiar house visitors in Europe and several parts of America, particularly in September when the summer brood rises from its hatching grounds in grassy lawns across the country. As they flutter about ceilings and lampshades, their legs dangling below them, many a stout-hearted Brit has been known to quail in the corner, nervously eyeing the trailing limbs, and recalling somewhere in the back of their minds that these insects are poisonous.

In fact, they're not. Like most members of the true fly family (*Diptera*, or 'two-winged'), craneflies are drinkers, living off

plant sap during their brief adult days. The confusion lies
in the fact that the cellar spider, an arachnid fond of darker
rooms whose presence is easily detected by its unusual strand-
like webs that appear untidy and incomplete, is also very
long-legged. And like some other spiders, the cellar spider is
indeed poisonous, although it is incapable of biting through
human skin so we have nothing whatsoever to fear from it.
Arachnologists have not helped matters either, giving the
minibeast the alternative name of the Daddy long-legs spider
because of its similarity to the cranefly.

So how can you tell the difference? Quite easily, really.
Craneflies have wings, long, thin abdomens and six legs. Cellar
spiders have rounded, waisted abdomens and eight legs. In
fact, their long legs apart, they really only have one similarity
in common – they are both completely harmless.

And in a similar vein...
The Daddy long-legs story doesn't end here.
Harvestmen, members of the arachnid family but
not actually spiders, are also sometimes called
Daddy long-legs. Often seen outdoors at the end
of the British summer, they have eight legs and an
unwaisted round abdomen. Despite the belief that
they, too, are poisonous, they are not.

The crocodile

It has been said that...

Crocodiles lure unsuspecting and sympathetic victims towards them by crying. Once within range, they strike and keep on crying as they rip off the do-gooder's flesh. This act gives rise to the phrase 'crocodile tears', meaning insincere sorrow.

The truth

'In that country and by all Ind be great plenty of cockodrills, that is a manner of a long serpent, as I have said before. And in the night they dwell in the water, and on the day upon the land, in rocks and in caves. And they eat no meat in all the winter, but they lie as in a dream, as do the serpents. These serpents slay men, and they eat them weeping.'

So wrote 'Sir John Maundeville' in the fictional fourteenth-century *The Travels of Sir John Maundeville*. This reptilian theory soon became accepted around the world, one sixteenth-century slaving crew reporting that crocs would 'cry and sobbe like a Christian body' to lure people in, while another belief had it that the tears were in sorrow that a man's head was too bony too eat. Even Shakespeare jumped on board: 'If that the earth could teem with woman's tears/Each drop she falls would prove a crocodile' (*Othello*). By the middle of the sixteenth century, the term 'crocodile's tears' had become part of British parlance.

In reality, crocodiles have special lachrymal glands that secrete fluids from behind their third eyelid, or nictating membrane. The purpose of these fluids is to help lubricate the eye when the cold-blooded creature, seeking the warmth of the sun, remains out of water for a while. Even from a distance, the heavily moistened eye of a croc – or indeed an alligator – is quite visible. Get a little closer (go on, dare you), and you can see the edge of the nictating membrane in the corner of the eye, just at the spot where a burgeoning tear might lie.

And in a similar vein...

Hollywood and adventure novels have often terrorised their audiences with tales of crocs and alligators chasing down their victims on land. No way. If you're reasonably fit (and you see the reptile coming), you can get away. The fastest speed clocked by a croc is just 10mph, and that was over just 30 yards before it tired.

The dog

It has been said that...

If you multiply a dog's age by seven you'll find its equivalent age in human terms.

The truth

We always like to anthropomorphise animal life, and get particularly carried away in the case of our pets. By comparing their life structures to our own, it helps us to feel closer to them. As a result, we've developed a rule of thumb for calculating how old a dog would be if it lived as long as humans (although dogs are probably delighted that they don't have to fill those extra decades by paying taxes, worrying about which car to buy, and discussing at length in which series *Frasier* went off the boil): we multiply its true age by seven.

The only trouble is, it doesn't work. To begin with, many breeds of dog are capable of conceiving around their first birthday – seven-year-old humans cannot make the same claim. At the other end of the scale, it's not at all unusual for a dog to make it into its late teens, whereas records of humans who've passed their 120th birthday are very thin on the ground. And you don't see many 60-year-olds sprinting round the garden like their eight-year-old dogs can still do. Different breeds have different life expectancies, too: border collies can live into their 20s, while bulldogs average around eight years' worth of life.

It's probably best just to call a four-year-old a four-year-old and leave it at that. But if you really feel the need to see how your pet is doing in its dotage, then the following approximation, devised by an American veterinary group, is probably the best to use: a one-year-old dog is about 15 human years old; 2=24, 3=32, 7=45, 10=56, 15=76, 20=98.

And in a similar vein...

Dogs only see in black and white. In actual fact, it's more complicated than that. The belief arose because dogs' eyes have more rod-shaped photoreceptors than cone-shaped, the latter allowing humans, for example, to see in colour. Recent research, however, has shown that although dogs may be colour-blind in the green and red areas of the spectrum, they can in fact distinguish shades of blue and purple, and can pick out yellow, too. How they interpret these shades is, of course, a matter of conjecture.

The duck

It has been said that...

A duck's quack doesn't echo, and no one really knows why.

The truth

This is one of those urban myths that has become standard trivia in quizzes everywhere. As urban myths can never really be proved to be true, the only thing to do is to prove them wrong.

The quack of a duck is no different to any other sound. Once emitted it travels through the air until it reaches the ear. Sounds have the ability to bounce off surfaces, such as mountains or walls, and change direction. As sound travels (at sea level) at the relatively slow speed of about 1,100 feet per second, it is possible to hear a sound directly from the source, and also a brief time later once it has bounced back from a reflective surface. This is an echo. The gap of time between hearing the sound directly, and its rebounding version, depends on how far away the 'bounce' occurs. As sounds can only travel limited distances, the further away the reflection, the louder the sound has to be to make it back. Similarly, if a sound reflects from a surface that is very close to the listener, it will return too quickly for the human ear to notice the difference.

The reason that ducks' quacks don't appear to echo is because, quite simply, they're rarely loud enough to travel the distance required for the human ear to appreciate the two separate sounds. Teams of scientists have in fact tested out this urban myth in chambers that can measure miniscule differences in sound reverberations, and have proved that the quack of a duck does in fact bounce off surfaces and is able to be heard more than once by sensitive equipment.

So that's another urban myth quacked.

And in a similar vein...

The maned goose of Australia gained its name because of the crest of feathers on its nape, and because it's not a particularly good swimmer, preferring to spend more of its time grazing along banks. Yet this rather goose-shaped bird is in fact a duck, one of the wood duck group that nests in trees. Which goes to show that if it looks like a goose, sounds like a goose and walks like a goose... it might still be a duck.

The elephant

It has been said that...

Elephants are afraid of mice.

The truth

Despite the fact that elephants had been well known to mankind for centuries, it is extraordinary how minimally we understood them by medieval times. According to bestiaries of the era, they live for 300 years, are afraid of mice, salute men and, having once lived in Africa and India, are now extinct in the former land. These records are all over the place. Elephants actually live for around 70 years or so, are very much still alive in Africa (despite the best efforts of the twentieth-century ivory hunters), and if anyone takes ear-flapping and trunk-waving as a salute and waves back, then they're in trouble.

The particularly interesting one, though, is the alleged anxiety around mice. Elephants have no such fear, as many a zookeeper who has watched mice scurry around the straw in elephant houses can attest. Elephants are sensitive creatures, and like most wild animals are wary of sounds and movements that they can't account for. The rustling of grasses in the savannah will catch an elephant's attention, and it is more likely to move away than investigate – although we're talking here about a level of rustling made by a sizeable animal such as a lion, rather than that made by something as small as a mouse.

The alleged fear of mice quite possibly derives from an ancient Roman warfare trick. Many of the Romans' enemies, notably Hannibal, used elephants as transport and weapons in their battles for their homeland, and it was recorded by writers like Pliny the Elder that the squeals of a pig thrust into an elephant's face would put it to flight. It was the squeal, not the pig, that upset the pachyderms, and over the centuries the legend grew – or minimised – so that elephants had become afraid of all high-pitched sounds... even the squeaks of a mouse.

And in a similar vein...

Elephants have no knee joints, so that if they fall down they can't get up again. They lean against a tree to sleep, so if you cut down that tree, over goes the elephant. These mistaken medieval beliefs probably comes from a misreading of Julius Caesar, who described elks, not elephants, in this manner. Elks or elephants – he was still wrong.

Garden birds

It has been said that...

You should feed garden birds only during the winter. Feeding them in the spring means they may give the wrong food to their young and kill them.

The truth

Today's garden bird-food industry is an extraordinary affair, turning over multi-millions each year as everything from choice seed mixes to squirrel-proof feeders gets snapped up by a public keen to attract birds to their gardens. Yet even now, there's room for expansion. When the British craze for feeding the birds on the doorstep first started to take off in the 1960s and 1970s, it was partly for the pleasure of seeing them from the comfort of your own kitchen window, and partly to help them survive harsh winters when food was scarce. As many species had been devastated during the long cold British winter of 1962/1963, (the wren population, for example, is believed to have fallen by as much as 75%), bird charities feared that some might not survive a second such disaster. The word went out: 'Feed the birds'.

But a second word went out, too: 'Only feed them in the winter'. The fear was that birds, suddenly discovering new sources of nutrition all year round, would feed unsuitable foodstuff to their nestlings. Baby blue tits would be choking to death on peanuts. Of course, birds are not really as stupid as that. They know what to feed their young by instinct, and given the choice of a peanut or an aphid, they'll munch the peanut themselves, and deliver the aphid to their offspring. In fact, by feeding the birds all year round on appropriate titbits, you can help the adults look after themselves while they're hunting to feed their families.

Many bird-food companies, in fact, now provide recommendations for ideal foodstuffs for every month of the year. It looks as if the industry is about to boom once more.

And in a similar vein...

Another garden visitor that's suffered from a popular food myth in recent times is the European hedgehog. A saucer of bread and milk is no nocturnal treat for them; it's actually a potential disaster. They struggle with milk's lactose content, which can cause diarrhoea, dehydration and even death. Much better to leave out a saucer of water instead.

The hare

It has been said that...

The English phrase 'Mad as a March hare' derives from the animal's craziness during the early months of spring.

The truth

'[Alice] walked on in the direction in which the March Hare was said to live. "I've seen hatters before," she said to herself; "the March Hare will be much the most interesting, and perhaps as this is May it won't be raving mad – at least not so mad as it was in March."'

The idea that hares go mad in March has been around far longer than Lewis Carroll's *Alice's Adventures in Wonderland* – it can be traced back at least to Chaucer, who referred to the animal's wildness. A century and a half later, the English playwright John Heywood, who was also a keen collector of proverbs and common sayings, gave the concept the phraseology we know today. In his book of proverbs, published in 1546, and alongside such recognisable entries as 'No man ought to looke a given horse in the mouth', 'Better one byrde in hand than ten in the wood', and 'A man may well bring a horse to the water, but he cannot make him drinke without he will', sits the legend 'Mad as a March hare'.

To be true, European brown hares do get very excitable as spring begins to blossom and bloom, but there's nothing mad about their antics. It's just the good old seasonal sex drive kicking in. The apparent dementia is in fact self-defence, as the females use their long forelegs to beat off the attentions of the males. The female American snowshoe hare goes even further, leaping out of the way of oncoming males, and sometimes urinating on them in the process.

The whole process gets the males even more excitable, and presumably encourages more successful mating. There's method in that madness, after all.

And in a similar vein...
The famous tales of Br'er Rabbit, as told by Uncle Remus, were not originally about a rabbit at all. They originated in Africa and were tales of the hare, whose cunning and speed got him out of tricky scrapes with jackals – later transmogrified into Br'er Fox.

The kingfisher

It has been said that...

Kingfishers can calm stormy seas in December simply by laying their eggs.

The truth

During winter months in Europe, common kingfishers, which generally live along riverbanks, often relocate to more coastal regions, including harbours and estuaries. This movement of the beautiful bird with a back reminiscent of spangly sunlit waters, coinciding as it sometimes does with a period of calm seas for about a fortnight around the winter solstice, led the ancients to believe that the seas relaxed their temperament for two weeks while the bird built its nest and laid its eggs on their surface.

Pliny the Elder pointed out that the calm period kicked in around the island of Sicily in particular, and Mediterranean sailors knew that this was the best time of the season – approximately between 15 and 29 December by today's calendar – to take to the sea.

They named this prosperous period 'halcyon days', after the Greek name for the kingfisher, which itself derives from *hals* and *kuon*, 'sea' and 'breed'. They even created a myth to explain it. When King Ceyx drowned at sea his wife Alcyone, daughter of Aeolus the god of winds, threw herself in after him in despair. The gods turned them into kingfishers out of pity, and Aeolus calmed the sea winds to allow them to build their family.

Of course the kingfisher does not breed during the winter, excavating holes in the sandy banks of fish-rich rivers and laying their eggs during the usual spring season.

And in a similar vein...
How did the common kingfisher get its
blue back and orange-red belly? According
to legend, it was the second bird set free by
Noah from the ark, but it flew too high, and
painted its back with the blue of the sky, and
burnt its breast with the heat of the sun.

The koala

It has been said that...

Koalas get high on the eucalyptus leaves that form their diet.

The truth

Koalas are picky eaters. Basically, if it doesn't say 'eucalyptus' on the tin, then it's not on the menu.

Nonetheless, being a eucalyptus eater does give you rather a useful ecological niche. The leaves of these many hundred species of tree (of which koalas eat a few dozen) are not particularly popular in the animal kingdom. They contain toxic oils, are difficult to chew and have very few calories, meaning that you need to have immunity to their poison to be able to eat them in the first place, and a most conservative lifestyle in order to make each calorie go a long way.

These the koala has in abundance. Special bacteria in their enlarged caecum (rather like an appendix) nullify the toxins that would destroy many other creatures, and enable digestion to take place, while their teeth are adapted for heavy-duty chewing: they grind the leaves down into a paste before swallowing.

It is their metabolic rate, however, which is most remarkable. It is extremely slow, allowing the chewed leaves to remain in the digestive system for as long as possible to extract the maximum nutrient content. It is so slow, in fact, that koalas need to sleep for up to 20 hours a day, so minimal is their energy. Koalas rarely drink water, either, getting the moisture they need from the leaves; 'koala' is an aboriginal term meaning 'non-drinker'.

So koalas aren't 'drugged' on the eucalyptus, they're just slow and sleepy in order to be able to eat it.

And in a similar vein...

Koalas are sometimes called koala bears, because of their similarity to teddy bears, but they're not related to that carnivore family at all. They're marsupials, and their closest living relatives are the equally Australasian wombats.

The lemming

It has been said that...

Lemmings control their populations by committing mass suicide over the edges of cliffs and riverbanks.

The truth

Walt Disney is responsible for many of the perceptions of animal life embedded in popular culture. To generations of avid movie-goers, Pluto is better known as a dog than a planet, the death of a deer's mother is the most tragic thing imaginable and everybody wants to be a cat. Yet sometimes the House of Mouse goes just a step too far, and never more so than in the 1958 film, *White Wilderness*.

The nature documentary purported to show animals of the northern climes living out their lives in tough conditions. One such animal was the lemming, and the film-makers had read that lemmings sometimes undergo mighty migrations in search of food, covering great tracts of land in their millions, searching for food as they go. In order to do this, they sometimes have to cross rivers, and some get swept away by the current. This, decided the producer, would make great watching! No matter that the migrations only take place every 30 years or so, or that none of the animals deliberately gets itself drowned, or that it's only the Norwegian lemmings, not the North American ones, that undertake such a journey. Let's film it anyway!

They bought some pet lemmings from a group of Inuit schoolchildren, filmed them on artificially snow-covered turntables in Alberta, and herded them safely over the edge, a sonorous voiceover proclaiming the rodents were deliberately hurling themselves off riverbanks to their doom.

Millions saw the film, assumed it to be true, and a legend was born.

And in a similar vein...

When Disney decided to film Rudyard Kipling's The Jungle Book, *he slipped in a few touches of his own. Bears can't sing, snakes can't hypnotise and vultures don't have Liverpool accents. The big one, however, was the introduction of a new character, King Louie. Great character, lousy geography. As Kipling could have told Disney, there are no orang-utans in India.*

The mayfly

It has been said that...

Mayflies only live for one day.

The truth

This is one that has to be qualified. Some species of mayfly live for a few months, others for over two years, but none lives for just one day.

None, that is, if we're looking at the entire lifespan of the insect. Mayflies spend the vast majority of their lives in an underwater form known as a nymph. Having hatched from eggs laid on or in the water, the nymph spends its time burrowing under the soft silt of a gently flowing stream, crawling along the riverbed, swimming free in waters with deep vegetation, or clinging to reeds in faster-flowing waters. During this time, they feed on algae as much as they can, try to avoid hungry amphibians, moult frequently as they grow, and generally live out their lives in great numbers in the running waters of the rivers of much of the world.

But they still have one last task to perform. To keep their species going, they must mate, and at the end of their months' or years' worth of sub-aquatic existence, they enter one final metamorphosis, emerging as a flying adult, or imago, for the final day of their lives. This winged version is a straightforward organism that does not eat and is too weak to crawl, but can fly in huge swarms and mate in midair. Once the job is done, the males have no further use for life, and often die that same day, while the females can live on for a few days in order to deposit their eggs in the most favourable place.

It's a brief adult life, it's true (and a virile one, to boot), but by insect standards, from hatch to dispatch, quite a lengthy one.

And in a similar vein...
They're called mayflies because they fly in May?
Some do, but many don't, and depending on the
species can emerge at almost any time of the year.
Some species even hatch three times a year.

The moth

It has been said that...

All butterflies fly by day, and all moths fly by night.

The truth

Butterflies are indeed diurnal creatures (although occasionally they will fly at night, particularly on migrations), emerging during the daylight hours, and becoming particularly active on warm and sunny days. But not all brightly coloured four-winged insects you see during the day are butterflies – some of them could be moths. At least 100 British species can be found during this time, and the stunningly beautiful sunset moth of Madagascar, one of the world's most splendid of creatures, can be found right up to the time of day from which it is named.

So if you come across a species with which you're unfamiliar, how can you tell if it's a butterfly or a moth? Truth is, there's really very little difference between the two. They're both members of the order *Lepidoptera* (which means 'scale-wing'), and both come in a bewildering array of shapes and colours. But many of the rules for telling them apart aren't quite watertight. Most butterflies rest with their wings open, and moths with their wings closed, but there are exceptions to each rule. Another frequent difference is that butterflies have clubbed antennae, whereas most (but be careful, not all) moths don't. If you can get up nice and close, meanwhile, and find a hook-like structure that joins the forewing to the hindwing, then you've almost definitely got yourself a moth: butterflies tend not to have them… but again, some do.

In short, there is no cast-iron way to tell the difference. The best thing you can do is to get to know all the butterflies in your country first, as there are far fewer of them, and then should you come across a species you don't know, then it must be a moth.

And in a similar vein…

Many people think that all moths eat clothing, but in truth only a tiny percentage of species do. And even then, it's not the adults themselves who tuck in to your fabric, but their larvae. By far, though, the vast majority of moth larvae are far happier with the right bit of greenery than an old sweater.

The opossum

It has been said that...

Opossums, the North American marsupials, can often be found hanging upside-down from trees holding themselves there only by their prehensile tails.

The truth

Opossums, the only marsupials found on the northern American continent, are real throwbacks to the early days of the mammal kingdom. First appearing about 80 million years ago towards the end of the Cretaceous period, they've settled into their omnivorous lifestyle very well, and adapted to the great influx of the human species to their lands better than most. Their name, incidentally, comes from the Algonquian 'apasum', which means 'white face'.

Although their tails are well-adapted tools that help them scale trees and get a good grip among the branches, they're nothing like strong enough to support the 9lb weight of a fully grown opossum. When the young are first born, however, they can grip onto branches with just their tails for perhaps a few seconds, but only tend to do so when they lose their balance while taking their early steps. The familiar cartoon image of opossums just hanging around upside-down in trees for no good reason other than that it seems like a comfy thing to do, is therefore a complete myth.

They do have one unusual trait, however, that they share only with humans and other primates, and that's a pair of opposable thumbs, which helps them further their arboreal habits. They've got one further trick, too: they're immune to most local snake poisons, ensuring that among the slugs, rats, fruit, insects and barbecue leftovers that make up an opossum's diet, snake is very high up on the menu.

And in a similar vein...

The phrase 'to play possum' means to deliberately lie low, to pretend to be incapacitated so as to avoid danger. Although it's true that a threatened opossum will indeed take on the appearance of death, deterring predators that are looking for live food, this is not a voluntary state. Fear throws the little animal into rigid shock, making this unusual defence mechanism one adopted not by choice.

The ostrich

It has been said that...

When under attack, ostriches bury their heads in the sand.

The truth

'To bury one's head in the sand' means to ignore a problem and hope that if you're not looking at it, it goes away. It comes from the popular belief that this is what ostriches do when they're under attack, but in reality, they don't (one reason is that there often isn't any sand around – ostriches are savannah birds, just as likely to be found in the open grasslands of Africa as any desert area). Nonetheless, ostriches do lay their necks along the ground when under threat, particularly if they're nesting birds, in the hope that the predator might think the humped body that they see is actually a termite mound or a small bush.

Despite this, it's still best to leave an ostrich alone. Threaten them, and they're as likely to attack back as they are to try to disguise themselves as part of the local flora.

Or they'll simply run away, and at a great rate, too. Their 12-foot strides can send them off at speeds of up to around 45mph, a pace they can keep up for several minutes. They carry their 200lb-plus weight on just two toes per foot, the only birds in the world to have so few – their cassowary, emu and rhea relatives can all boast three.

The camel also has two toes per foot, which is part of the reason why the ostrich bears the scientific name *Struthio camelus*: the long eyelashes, the ability to withstand harsher climates, and their overall large size have also helped contribute to this comparison.

And in a similar vein...

Early Christian visitors to Africa believed that ostriches didn't brood their eggs, but stared at them intensely, the heat from their gaze warming the eggs until they hatched. The belief probably arose from the attentive protection an adult ostrich gives to its young, and in some orthodox Mediterranean churches today, ostrich eggs are still displayed as a symbol of a person's need to protect his soul at all times.

The owl

It has been said that...

Owls are among the cleverest of birds, their learning capacity is great and their wisdom a shining example to us all.

The truth

There are various ways of measuring intelligence in birds. The facility of play is one sign, and members of the crow family such as ravens have this in abundance. Then there's the ability to learn, which many perching birds, and pigeons and doves, have frequently been proven to do. The power of mimicry, such as parrots and mynahs possess, is seen by some as an indication of a good brain. Owls do none of these things to any extent.

The nocturnal species spend much of the day squatting on a branch blinking down at the frantic life below and moving barely a feather. And this is why the owl has been accredited with intelligence – where most birds look at you side-on, the owl's large eyes gaze directly at you, taking you in, assessing you, and then its head swivels round to face completely the opposite direction to start contemplating something else. Such apparent nonchalant condescension, such perceived steady consideration, is what has given the birds their credibility. Even Athena, the Greek goddess of wisdom, was always pictured in the company of a little owl. In reality, owls are no more intelligent than most birds, and a good bit less so than some.

What they are very good at, though, is using their senses to hunt silently in the dead of night like few other birds can. They have found an ecological niche, and exploited it to the full.

Now that is clever.

And in a similar vein...

Owls are not symbols of wisdom everywhere in the world. In India, for example, their nocturnal nature has given them status as ill omens and unthinking servants of the dead. To call someone 'an owl' in that country is to suggest they are a fool.

The panda

It has been said that...

The giant panda, despite sometimes being called the panda
bear, is not actually a bear at all, but is more closely related
to raccoons.

The truth

While steadily diminishing in the wild ever since it was first
described by Western science in 1869, the giant panda, has
been bounced back and forth by scientists from bear to
raccoon family ever since.

First described as a bear by its Western discoverer Père
David, this theory was rapidly challenged when the creature
was studied more carefully. Several aspects of the panda's
make-up share more similarities with another creature, the red
panda, than with bears, such as its skull, teeth, forepaws and
genitalia, as well as its fondness for bamboo. As the red – or
lesser – panda has long been allied with the raccoons, the giant

panda was moved accordingly into this group. But the debate continued. Although the 'not-a-bear' camp held most of the trump cards, the 'is-a-bear' brigade kept up their research. All the while, the general public perception was that the panda, although bear-like, was not actually a bear.

In the 1980s, DNA evidence was investigated, which seemed to suggest that pandas shared more in common with bears than raccoons. More molecular work was done in the following years, and in the late 1990s, the complete scientific evidence was brought together in one study, which concluded that the panda is indeed a member of the bear family, branching off much earlier – perhaps 22 million years ago – than the other seven extant species. As for the red panda, the jury is out. Some consider it a lone species of its kind, some link it still with raccoons, while others yet still relate it most closely to bears. It is likely that more twists are to come before the mystery of the pandas is fully resolved.

And in a similar vein...

Although the Western world has only known about pandas for a century and a half, the Chinese have, of course, long been familiar with them. Many thousands of years ago, they believed they had magical powers that could ward off natural threats. Unfortunately, however, it appears these powers are unable to cope with the man-made threats of habitat destruction.

The parrot

It has been said that...

Parrots are prone to great bouts of depression, hence the
British phrase 'sick as a parrot', meaning to be completely and
utterly fed up... normally because your football team has lost.

The truth

True, some caged birds do react badly to confinement, but
they are just as likely to become agitated or violent, as they
are to become withdrawn. The main illness suffered by
parrots is down to the bacterium *Chlamydia psittaci* that
causes the distressing condition psittacosis. Infected birds
are likely to suffer from diarrhoea, weight loss, shivering fits
and sleepiness.

During the 1970s, a few cases of human psittacosis were reported in British tourists returning from trips to West Africa. Suffering anything from flu-like symptoms to severe pneumonia, the victims' tales hit the nation's headlines for a while, and the phrase 'sick as a parrot' was briefly a topical way of saying 'sick as a dog', to mean that someone was really badly run down. By the time the British football community discovered the phrase, the meaning had simplified to no more than a general state of the blues, and had become standard football-speak for: 'I can't believe I scored an own goal/the ref gave a penalty/we wuz robbed.'

There is another English footballing theory in some parts of West London that the phrase goes back much further, though. When Tottenham Hotspur toured South America for a football tournament in 1909, they adopted a parrot which they took back to London with them. According to Spurs fans, the parrot died 10 years later on the very day when bitter rivals Arsenal replaced them in the first division in 1919.

And in a similar vein...

Many birds suffering from psittacosis are put down, their owners believing that the illness is terminal. It is not, and can be cured with appropriate treatment and disinfection, applied for about 45 days.

The penguin

It has been said that...

Penguins fall over on their backs while watching planes flying overhead.

The truth

This particular belief gained momentum in the 1980s as reports came through that pilots stationed at the Falkland Islands after the crisis between Britain and Argentina in 1982, would amuse themselves by flying above penguin rookeries (colonies). The penguins would watch them so intently, that they would fall over backwards and not be able to get up again.

To begin with, penguins are far more flexible than this myth would suggest – many species leap in and out of the sea during the breeding season, and are used to landing in all kinds of awkward positions from which they're able to right themselves. The 'can't get up' part of the story is easily debunked.

But what about the plane-watching? Could it be possible that the birds are so fascinated by these curious flying objects that they overstretch themselves and tumble? The myth had gained such credibility after a couple of decades that the British Antarctic Survey team decided to test it out in 2000. Pilots spent a full month in Antarctic Bay zipping back and forth over king penguin rookeries. All the birds did was go quiet while the intruders flew past, while some younger ones waddled away from the disturbance. Not a single one fell over.

Unlike the penguins themselves, this is one urban legend that when put to the test, simply doesn't stand up.

And in a similar vein...

The penguin probably gets its name because the first explorers to discover it thought it was related to what they already called a 'penguin', but which we now call the great auk, a flightless bird, now extinct, which it closely resembled. Penguins are in fact more closely related to albatrosses, petrels and even pelicans. And why was the great auk known as a penguin in the first place? There are three theories: that the name derived from the Welsh 'pen gwyn' (white head); that it comes from its flightlessness or 'pinned wing'; or that the Latin 'pinguis', meaning 'fat', was used to describe the bird's extra fat deposits that protected it from the cold. Take your pick.

The porcupine

It has been said that...

Porcupines can fire their quills at predators, inflicting nasty damage, and ensuring that they're not attacked again.

The truth

The quills of a porcupine can indeed cause great pain and injury to the over-curious, but they certainly can't be fired from the body. Quills are actually no more than hardened hairs with sharp barbed tips, and porcupines can no more use them as projectiles than we can our own hair.

They are, however, a magnificent protection system. When confronted by a creature that makes the porcupine feel uncomfortable, it simply turns its back on it and wanders off. Should the creature – say, a young bobcat or a feral dog – start to follow, the porcupine starts to back up into the potential predator's quivering nose. Once a sharp quill has struck home, it becomes embedded in the flesh, and releases itself from the porcupine's own body. Anyone watching a porcupine swing its tail at a predator, and seeing the larger animal recoil in pain with quills emerging from its face, could easily get the impression that the quills had been fired.

It can take several months for porcupines to regrow their quills, but this isn't a problem. They have about 30,000 in the first place. Amazingly, young porcupines, or porcupettes, acquire their quills very quickly. They can't be born with them – their mothers would probably not survive the eye-watering experience – but the quills are able to harden within a mere 30 minutes of birth.

The quills also give porcupines means of flight as well as fight. They enable their bearer to get a good grip in trees, where they can often be seen tucked up on branches looking rather like large nests. In addition, as the quills are hollow, their buoyancy allows the creatures to swim.

And in a similar vein...
Because of their sharp exteriors, many people think of porcupines as being related to hedgehogs, their apparent European counterparts. Not so. Porcupines are herbivorous rodents, whereas hedgehogs are insectivores, related to moles and shrews.

Scientific names

NOTIOCRYPTORRHYNCHUS PUNCTATOCARINULATUS

It has been said that...

The scientific names given to animals are always serious, complicated and difficult to remember.

The truth

Well, to be fair, some are. It's a damn sight easier to say 'weevil' than it is to utter the scientific name of one of its family members, *Notiocryptorrhynchus punctatocarinulatus*. And most people would feel more comfortable slipping 'stratiomyid fly' into the conversation, than attempt its more accurate name *Parastratiosphecomyia stratiosphecomyioides*.

But not all scientific names are as daunting as these mighty tongue-twisters. The world of biology, just as in most industries, has its fair share of jokers, and over the years they've had quite a bit of fun with the vagaries of official Linnean nomenclature. Witness, for example, the braconid first identified in 1993 as a new species within the genus *Heerz*. It was given the specific, or 'second', name of *lukenatcha*. Now say those two words together. See? Try saying out loud, too, the species of tortricid moth known as *Eubetia bigaulae*, or the water beetle *Ytu brutus*, or the Fijian snail *Ba humbugi*.

Biologists have shown over the years an interest in film and literature, too. A dolichopodid fly which in death tends to splay its feet outwards tramps through life with the name *Campsicnemius charliechaplini*, while a pterosaur found in the rainforests of Brazil, and similar to that described in the dinosaur novel *The Lost World*, pays homage to that book's author by being named *Arthurdactylus conandoylensis*. One wonders, though, how it came to be a spider not a bat that ended up with the name *Draculoides bramstokeri*.

And here's a quick tip for anyone who can't get their tongue around the phrase 'mythicomyiid flies'. Just think of the scientific name of one of them. It is, quite simply, a *Pieza kake*.

And in a similar vein...

Many people think that scientific names tend to be pretty lengthy, as well as complicated. Again, not always. The common swift comes in at just eight letters, Apus apus, *as does the lion,* Felis leo. *The shortest of the lot, however, belongs to the great evening bat of Vietnam – or Ia io.*

The shark

It has been said that...

Sharks are frequent killers, and among the most dangerous creatures on the planet.

The truth

In the 15 years up until 2004, a total of 90 fatal shark attacks were recorded by the International Shark Attack File – that's an average of six per year. Bear in mind that that's a global figure, and so compares very favourably with the 4.8 people killed every year just in the UK – by cows! Compare, too, with the fact that dogs kill 16 people every year in the United States alone. In even greater contrast, 18 people are killed each year by tractors – and that's just in Kentucky! (Note: do not try to cage, feed or pet tractors. Despite their brief appearance in this book, they are not animals.)

We're actually pretty safe at sea from shark attacks – of the 400 species of shark around the world, only 10 have ever been recorded as attacking humans. And even those 10 are predators mainly of fish, and will not attack humans if not provoked. So why do fatal shark attacks, despite their infrequency, grab the headlines?

Hollywood films apart, it's all to do with the water. Humans are comparatively helpless at sea, and sharks are most definitely not, so the fear centres around our sense of vulnerability in an environment to which we're not best suited. This fear can reach irrational levels: selachophobia – fear of sharks – is a recognised medical condition, suffered by people who don't even live near the sea, but for whom just the knowledge that sharks are out there somewhere is very debilitating. Selachophobes worry that their loved ones might be in danger somewhere, and they're even afraid of taking baths.

The shark becomes a symbol of threat in a world in which you feel you have no control.

And in a similar vein...
If you do find yourself all at sea with an aggressive
shark, you just punch it on the nose, don't you? Well,
best not. Like any other creature, you're really only
likely to anger it more. If you can poke it in the eye,
you'll stand a better chance of getting away.

The snake

It has been said that...

Snakes hypnotise their prey before striking.

The truth

Here's some advice: never try to win some quick cash by
entering a staring contest with a snake. You'll get fleeced.
Snakes, you see, have no movable eyelids, and even in sleep
their eyes are always open, covered only by a transparent scale
that provides protection against water and the elements. This
scale, or spectacle, is shed along with the rest of the snake's
skin, and some palaeontologists add it to their evidence that
snakes evolved from aquatic dinosaurs such as the mosasaur.

Understandably, this staring appearance has given rise to the
idea that snakes hypnotise their prey into immobility. Some

people, however, have tried to suggest that the hypnotic role can be reversed, most notably the snake-charmers of India. Sitting cross-legged on the ground before a king cobra, their pipe-playing apparently tames the beast, and sets it a-swaying to the music.

In reality, snakes do not hear the way that we do, and are more sensitive to vibration than to sound. Nonetheless, a 'charmed' snake is actually responding to visual stimuli, not aural. As the snake-charmer plays, he moves his pipe up and down and around, and the snake, whose visual perception is not too strong, weaves with it in order to keep it within eyeshot. And why doesn't the charmer get bitten? The cobra's raised posture, hood spread, is more defensive than aggressive, and the charmer sits just far enough away to remain out of striking distance.

And although some charmers treat their snakes pretty well, others aren't so diligent, even removing the animal's fangs just to be on the safe side.

And in a similar vein...
All snakes lay eggs, right? Actually, only about
70% of them do. Some species, such as the British
adder or the garter snakes of North America bear
their young live, the offspring having hatched from
their eggs within their mothers' bodies.

The spider

It has been said that...

A species of spider, rare and venomous, lives in the tunnels below the Queen's residence at Windsor Castle.

The truth

In 2001, a story broke on the British, as well as some of the international press, that was guaranteed to startle. 'Nests of rare venomous spiders have been found near Windsor Castle,' gasped the BBC, breathlessly, 'and could be living under the royal estate itself.' Discovered by British Telecom engineers who were laying new cables underground, the 'facts' did indeed seem most disturbing. A 3.5-inch legspan was quoted, as were jaws big enough to puncture human flesh, and as there was a possibility that the species was rare or even previously considered extinct, they would automatically become a protected species. Watch out your majesty! God save the Queen!

Well, there's nothing like tapping into the deep well of arachnophobia to sell a story. A few days after the scaremongering facts were disseminated, some proper arachnologists came in for a look. They soon discovered that the animal was nothing more than *Meta menardi*, the European cave spider, which is not rare or even endangered, is not at all dangerous and is about half the size as was originally claimed.

Thanks to shoddy and speculative reporting, an urban legend had been born, one which still travels the internet today. Just goes to show that when it comes to spiders, you shouldn't believe everything you read on the web.

And in a similar vein...

Another spider-related urban legend of recent years concerns the revelation that the poisonous South American blush spider hides under aeroplane and airport toilet seats. The tale is a hoax. Not only does the spider not exist, but neither, too, do the airport, the doctor or the medical association quoted in the story.

The toad

It has been said that...

It's best not to handle a toad, because it can give you warts.

The truth

Warts are caused by a virus, not an amphibian. The virus in question – the human papillomavirus – settles in the epidermis and replicates itself, creating a benign tumour. The virus can be spread through contact, however, which is why the toad, with its wart-like bumps on its body, has often thought to have been a conduit of the minor ailment. These bumps, however, contain no papillomavirus. Two major bumps, called paratoid glands, can be found just behind the eyes and are part of the toad's defence system. They contain a fatty toxic substance – bufagin – that is designed to deter predators, particularly useful when you don't have the hopping power of a frog to escape with.

Although the glands are there to deter snakes, foxes and the like, they also drew plenty of attention from superstitious medieval types who, viewing them as remnants of demonic horns, decided that they must be creatures with satanic associations. This was good news for the toad as folk were loth to harm them for fear of inciting the wrath of Old Nick.

Witches, however, took a different approach, using toads as part of their satanic worship in all sorts of lotions and potions, and even believing that the great horned one himself would appear to them in the amphibian's form. One recipe, which enabled witches to fly, was especially gruesome. It involved boiling together the ashes of a toad along with a Christian's powdered bones, the blood of a child and, presumably to take the edge off, mixed herbs.

And in a similar vein...

As recently as the eighteenth century, toads were believed to cause epilepsy simply by staring at you. The French historian Abbé Rousseau, for example, reported that when he looked into a toad's eyes he fell into a fainting fit. Perhaps this was the result of a disturbed mind rather than amphibian evil – in 1784, the good abbot shot himself.

The tortoise

It has been said that...

Giant tortoises, such as those from the Galapagos islands, can live for over 200 years.

The truth

Rather a hard one to make a call on, is this. Come back in a few decades, and there'll be an answer for you. The fact is that it's quite possible that giant tortoises can survive for more than two centuries – it's just that we haven't known about them properly for long enough to find out!

The closest we've come to proof of such longevity is a tortoise from Madagascar that was presented to the Queen of Tonga by Captain Cook in the mid-1770s, and which died in 1965. The animal was said to be fully grown at the time of capture, although there is no documentation to prove this. Consequently, although it could have lived well beyond 200 years, we only know that it lived for at least 188 of them.

Perhaps the best known of all the giant tortoises, though, is Harriet, who lives in Australia Zoo, Brisbane. Her fame is due to the belief that Charles Darwin brought her back from the Galapagos islands where he found her in 1835, although recent research, in particular by micropalaeontologist Paul Chambers, suggests that this was not the case. There is not enough accurate paperwork to prove that she was one of the four tortoises brought back in the *Beagle*, and most damningly, her subspecies does not live on the islands that Darwin visited.

Nonetheless, documentation shows that she was at least around in 1850, so should she live until 2050, we would have our first confirmed case of a bicentennial birthday.

And in a similar vein...

Tortoises can't kill you, right? Wrong. According to Greek history, the dramatist Aeschylus was killed when an eagle dropped a tortoise on his head, mistaking his bald pate for a rock on which the reptile's hard shell might break. History does not record what happened to the tortoise.

CHAPTER 2

Mystifying misnomers

In which we meet some poor creatures that have
been saddled with ridiculous names

The barnacle goose

It has been said that...

Barnacle geese are hatched not from eggs, but barnacles.

The truth

The barnacle goose and the goose barnacle: two completely different creatures with very similar names. But then, there was a time when British folk thought that the bird and the crustacean were one and the same, the former being the adult version of the latter.

It was perhaps an easy mistake to make. To begin with, the goose barnacle with its grey-white shell edged with black and its stalk that anchors it to rocks, does look rather like a goose's head and neck. In addition, as migration was a poorly understood subject in the sixteenth century, people needed an answer to the vexed question of why the barnacle goose, an overwintering bird from Greenland, was never seen during the summer months. As birds in general appear from eggs – oval objects with hard shells – then why shouldn't this particular goose appear from a watery version of such an object?

But then, perhaps the mistake wasn't quite as innocent as it might seem. As a result of this erroneous belief, the barnacle goose had become rather a handy bird. The Catholic faith forbade the eating of flesh during Lent and Fridays, but the goose, thanks to its apparent marine origins, could rather conveniently be classified as fish. Anyone who ate the bird and noticed its close resemblance to other poultry in taste and texture were probably just encouraged to shut up and keep chewing.

And in a similar vein...

The brent goose, another wintering visitor to Britain, was also believed to have emerged from barnacles. Where the barnacle goose owes its English name to this theory, the brent goose's bizarre origins are commemorated in its scientific name: Branta bernicla.

The buffalo

It has been said that...

Buffaloes are huge herbivores with shaggy manes that once roamed the great American plains in vast numbers.

The truth

What's the difference between a buffalo and a bison? You can't wash your hands in a buffalo.

OK, sorry about that. The real answer, when talking about the great beasts of America, and when being technical, is that one exists and the other does not. The shaggy animal that once covered the plains in tens of millions, before being slaughtered in the mid-nineteenth century at the rate of about 200,000 per year for its pelt and meat until only 300 remained, is the bison. Even its scientific name – the easily remembered *Bison bison* – should leave no one in any doubt. Yet Americans call it a buffalo. Why?

The answer comes from the early French explorers who initially named the bison '*le boeuf*' for its meaty qualities. The name transmogrified first into 'buffle' and finally into buffalo once the English got there. And buffalo it remained, despite the fact that its closest relative, found in Poland, Romania, Russia and Ukraine, is known as the European bison.

And what of buffaloes? You'll need to visit Asia or Africa to see these, the former for water buffaloes, anoas and tamaraws, the latter for the cape buffalo.

And in a similar vein...
There are several other American creatures named
by the pioneers of the New World because they
reminded the travellers of the familiar animals of
home. The bird world is particularly rife with these
anomalies: the American robin with its red breast
is actually a thrush, the buzzard is a vulture, the
red-winged blackbird is a New World oriole, the
American redstart is really a New World warbler...
the list goes on.

The cuckoo

It has been said that...

Grasshoppers are born from the saliva of cuckoos.

The truth

Cuckoo-spit does indeed result in small hopping creatures, but then cuckoo-spit isn't what it proclaims to be. It is the creation of the froghopper, a small meadow insect related to the aphids, which has a remarkable self-protection plan. In its nymph, or larval, stage it mixes a secretion rather like egg white with droplets of plant sap to create a frothy substance in which it hides until ready to emerge as an adult. And what an adult it turns into! Despite its tiny size, it's able to jump as high as 27in, further than any other creature in proportion to its size.

There's no doubt that these collections of frothy cuckoo-spit (as they're still known), which can be found in great quantities on spring-time plant stems in Europe, look like salival deposits, but why were they thought to have come from the European cuckoo? The answer lies in timing and size. As the bubbly substances first appear at about the time that the bird begins to arrive in Europe and start calling, it was thought that as cuckoos were pretty much the only migratory birds large enough to create spitballs of such a size, they must be the culprits. And when observers saw small insects emerging a few weeks later and hopping off like grasshoppers, the erroneous connection was complete.

The cuckoo flower also derives its name from its coincidental flowering upon the arrival of the bird, while several counties in England hold cuckoo days in late April to celebrate the first hearing of its iconic call.

And in a similar vein...
The cuckoo, perhaps because of its parasitic
habit of having other birds bring up its young, was
once thought to be a lazy migrator, too. Isidore of
Seville, the seventh-century nature chronicler, was
among many who believed they came to Europe
from Africa on the backs of kites.

The eagle

It has been said that...

The bald eagle is so named because its white head gives it a
featherless look from a distance.

The truth

It seems strange that the very feathers that help give this
American bird such an iconic status should be deemed not to
be there at all, according to its name. A vulture, now that's
definitely a baldy, its lack of head feathers enabling it to dig
deep into bloody carcasses without clogging itself up. The
bald eagle, however, has a head quite unmistakably cloaked in
magnificent white. So how did it get its name? The answer lies
in the vicissitudinous nature of the English language.

In Middle English, if you wanted to describe something as being shining white, or as having a white patch, you would say that it was 'balled', deriving from the word 'ball' meaning 'white patch'. Eventually, this word contracted into 'bald', and became associated with the white patch of scalp that shines through a mat of hair on a person's head. Today, we don't use the word to describe whiteness: the bald eagle's own scientific name is *Haliaeetus leucocephalus*, meaning quite literally 'white-headed sea eagle', not a featherless reference in sight.

Bald or not, the eagle has had a chequered career over the years. It became the national bird of the US back in 1782, but was still hunted for many years by fishermen with whom it competed. It was finally given protection in 1940 under the grandiosely titled National Emblem Act, although its numbers continued to plummet, thanks to the use of the DDT pesticide which got into the bird's diet and weakened the shells of its eggs. The banning of DDT has helped lift the population from a low of about 400 pairs to around 6,000 today.

And in a similar vein...
Another bird has become forever associated with baldness – to be as 'bald as a coot' means to have no hair at all, but the term derives from the bird's white frontal shield, or white patch.

Flying mammals

It has been said that...

In addition to bats, there are various types of mammals that can fly, such as the flying squirrel and the flying mouse.

The truth

Birds do it. Bees do it. But educated fleas don't do it, and neither, with the exception of bats, do mammals. Fly, that is. Some mammals, however, have become very adept at gliding, having evolved large folds of skins between the limbs on either sides of their bodies which work as parachutes and enable them to coast through the air from tree to tree.

There are many species of them in various countries across the world, and they're a magnificent sight, as anyone who watched David Attenborough's BBC TV series *The Life of Mammals* will testify. In fact, in preparation for the programme, the production team wanted to film in North America one of the so-called flying squirrels feeding from the presenter's hand. To try to get the creatures accustomed to the idea, they rigged up a scarecrow with a cardboard cutout of David's head and a plate of food, and just left it there. Unfortunately, it didn't work. A bear knocked 'David' down, and rather unceremoniously disrobed the great man.

But back to the science. In the classification system of the natural world there's an entire order given over to just two of these creatures. The order *Dermoptera*, which means 'skin-winged', comprises just the pair of flying lemurs found in the Far East: one in the Philippines, the other from Java to Borneo. Among the largest of all the gliding mammals, they can travel up to 500 feet with one leap.

And in a similar vein...

Flying lemurs are double misnamed. Not only do they not fly, they're not lemurs either, but an independent branch of mammalian evolution, possibly from a primate ancestor, or maybe even with an insectivorous background, even though they're actually herbivores. Confusing? Probably better just to call them by their local name – colugo.

The giraffe

It has been said that...

The giraffe is the offspring of the camel and the leopard.

The truth

The scientific name of the giraffe bears testament to a huge, but understandable, misunderstanding. *Giraffa camelopardalis*, as it is still known, was first exhibited in captivity by Julius Caesar in 46BC at Rome. This was the first time that the giraffe had been seen by Europeans, other than travellers who had brought back stories of a creature that must be a hybrid, its masticating mouth, long neck and manner of walking coming from a camel as a mother, and its spots derived from its father, a leopard.

Yet Caesar's exhibit, and future captive individuals, brought doubt to the minds of some early naturalists. Realising that the beast's docile temperament bore little resemblance to either parent, Pliny the Elder put forward a different view: 'The Ethiopians give the name of *nabun* to one animal', he wrote, 'that has a neck like a horse, feet and legs like an ox, and a head like a camel, and is of a ruddy colour picked out with white spots, owing to which it is called a camelopardalis. It has subsequently been recognised to be more remarkable for appearance than for ferocity, and consequently it has received the name of *ovis ferae* (wild sheep).'

Well, Pliny also got it wrong – the giraffe is not a sheep, either. It's more closely related to deer and cattle than sheep, although its closest living relative is the okapi, which was only discovered by the Western world in 1901. The word 'giraffe', incidentally, comes from the Arabic word for the animal: *zaràfa*.

And in a similar vein…

The giraffe's long neck is perhaps the most famous example of misunderstood evolution. The French biologist Lamarck, in the early nineteenth century, believed that as individual giraffes stretched their necks to reach leaves high on acacia trees, their necks became slightly longer, a characteristic which they passed on to their offspring. Darwin's theories and the understanding of genetics have since debunked inheritance of acquired characteristics as a means of evolution.

The kangaroo

It has been said that...

The word 'kangaroo' is an aboriginal term meaning 'I don't know what you mean', the answer given to Captain Cook and his men in 1770 when they first asked what the bounding creature was.

The truth

Delightful though it would be for this myth to be true, it is sadly not. The word 'kangaroo' does not exist in any extant aboriginal language, but in 1898, an ethnologist called WE Roth wrote a letter to *The Australasian* pointing out that in Guugu Yimidhirr, a language in the Endeavour River area, he had discovered that the animal was called 'gaNurru'. This, he stated, was probably the phrase that Cook had heard and transcribed incorrectly over a century previously. The letter was published, but missed by lexicographers, and so the idea that the animal had been named after a simple misunderstanding persisted. It was only in 1972, when the anthropologist John Haviland was studying the language, that the word came to light again.

So the amusing derivation of 'kangaroo' seems to be just an urban myth after all. The story behind the meaning of 'indri', however, is not. The indri is a large Madagascan lemur with an eerie call, and is known in Malagasy as the babakoto. In 1780, the traveller Pierre Sonnerat (the first Westerner, incidentally, to give a scientific description of the lychee) was visiting Madagascar, when the lemur suddenly appeared in the trees. 'Indri, indri!' called out his guide in Malagasy. 'Look, look.'

And in a similar vein...

Many agricultural Australians consider kangaroos to be pests, destructive of wheat crops and competitive with sheep in grazing areas. This sort of argument is often used in support of kangaroo hunting. In fact research has shown that kangaroos rarely visit wheat farms – only 5% are affected by them – and that red kangaroos, supposedly among the most pestilent, have no effect whatsoever on sheep flocks.

The mammoth

It has been said that...

Mammoths are still with us today, living under the ground like giant moles, and dying when they surface into the light.

The truth

We now know that woolly mammoths, the great elephantine beasts of the Ice Age, died out about 11,000 years ago. We know this because we've got a grip on what extinction is all about, but it's a concept that is fairly new to human understanding of the world. A few centuries ago, most people assumed that any animals that had ever lived probably still lived, so any remains they might find must belong to creatures still extant. So how did they explain the mighty mammoth corpses and bones that they would often find, frozen in the tundra expanses of Siberia, when living representatives of this huge species were never to be seen? The conclusion: they must live underground. The theory was that below the earth dwelled giant tunnelling beasts that depended for their existence on dark conditions. Should an unfortunate individual accidentally tunnel its way to the surface, it would die immediately upon contact with the sunlight and air. This explained the frozen and well-preserved corpses often found protruding above the ground.

And so they gave these animals a name. It appears they named it 'earth mole', which in Ostyak, the Russian tongue of the time and region, translated as 'manimut'. Thus it is that our modern word 'mammoth' appears to be based on a small, tunnelling creature. Talk about making mountains out of molehills.

And in a similar vein...

Another early theory to explain the existence of mammoth bones was that they were the remnants of ancient giants, such as the sea monster Cetus that was slain by Perseus, or the 19-foot tall Cimbrian king Teutobochus. In addition, as mammoth skulls have a mighty hole where the trunk was once attached, they might have been the inspiration for the legendary one-eyed Cyclops.

The prairie dog

It has been said that...

There exists in the prairies of North America a species of wild
dog that burrows underground and eats grass.

The truth

They don't look like dogs, they don't act like dogs, so why are
prairie dogs, those sociable little rodents of the Great Plains of
America, so-called? The answer lies in the voice. The chipmunk-
like creatures emit a barking sound that early pioneers decided
reminded them of man's best friend. To be honest, it takes rather
a stretch of the imagination to compare the chirping yips of a
prairie dog with the bark of even the smallest terriers, but then
many of those old-timers had very elastic imaginations indeed.

Having said that, the vocalisations of the prairie dog are
actually rather complex. One biologist, Con Slobodchikoff,

even suggests that they have a very varied language, comprising nouns, verbs and adjectives. He discovered that the prairie dog warning call when a man approached in a green shirt was different to when he approached in a yellow shirt, and when he showed different individuals pictures of a European owl that they had not seen before, they all piped up with the same new call.

Slobodchikoff has logged well over 100 prairie dog 'words' in his research, and has even detected regional dialects in the rodents. As prairie dogs are sociable animals, relying on each others' senses for survival from predators, they may have developed such subtle inflexions in a call to help make the difference between knowing that the threat comes from above, in the shape of a hawk, or from the ground, in the shape of a coyote.

So maybe those prairie dogs first spotted by hunting pioneers weren't sounding like dogs at all. Maybe they were saying 'dog'.

And in a similar vein...

Many consider prairie dogs to be pests, multiplying rapidly like rabbits before burrowing underground and destroying agricultural areas. In fact, the rodents only breed once a year, and normally have a litter of just three or four pups.

The reindeer

It has been said that...

Reindeer are so called because for many centuries, peoples of
northern lands have used them to pull their sledges.

The truth

Many a child grows up with the image emblazoned on their
mind of Santa Claus and his reindeer-drawn sleigh sweeping
across the Christmas Eve skies. And as those children grow
up and find out what the word 'rein' means in the context of
domesticated animals, they could be forgiven for thinking that
this was how the great deer of the snows got its name.

The truth is more bizarre. The reindeer has been known
long before the English language shaped itself into its current
format, and was given the name 'hreinn' in Old Norse, possibly
in mimicry of its call. So, if 'hreinn' was the name given to the
reindeer, then 'reindeer' effectively means 'reindeer-deer'.

And then it gets a little more confusing. Back before the fourteenth century, deer in England weren't called deer at all, but 'heorot'. The word 'deer' actually meant 'animal', and came to be used exclusively for the antlered creatures as the fifteenth century rolled on, mainly because the much-loved sport of hunting had made them everyone's animal of choice. Even Shakespeare still made use of this coinage, writing in King Lear of 'mice, and rats, and such small deer'. All of which explains that reindeer actually means 'reindeer-animal'.

Perhaps it's best just to use the American term, and call it a caribou. It's an Algonquin word meaning 'snow-scraper'.

And in a similar vein...

Donner and Blitzen were two of Santa's reindeer, right? Well, not originally. The poem 'A Visit from Saint Nicholas', first published in 1823, names Santa's eight reindeer as: Dasher, Dancer, Prancer, Vixen, Comet, Cupid, Dunder and Blixem. The poem was written by Henry Livingston, a New Yorker of Dutch descent, who gave the final two creatures the Dutch names of 'thunder and lightning'. Over the years, as Dutch became less well-known, the names transmogrified, and had become the German forms Donner and Blitzen by the time Gene Autry was singing about their new friend Rudolph in 1949.

The rhino

It has been said that...

The white rhino and the black rhino are so named because of their colours.

The truth

There are a number of differences between the two species of African rhino, but colour is hardly one of them. Put two individuals next to each other, and you'd struggle to say which is darker than the other. You'd be forgiven for thinking that they should both be called the 'brownish-grey rhino'.

But then the great beasts didn't get their names because of their colour. One of the biggest distinctions between the two is their upper lip, which is squared-off in the case of the white rhino, and hooked in the case of the black. These types of lips enable the two species to attack different types of vegetation. The blunt lip of the white rhino is ideal in helping the creature graze, while the black rhino uses its narrower, more prehensile lip to tug at leaves and shoots.

When the Dutch first arrived in southern Africa, they noted the broad, square upper lip of the former species, and named it accordingly. The 'wijde' rhino, or 'wide' rhino, soon contracted to 'white' rhino, once the English started to move in. Purely because it wasn't the white rhino, the black rhino was simply named in contrast.

The word 'rhinoceros' itself is a more accurately descriptive name. It comes from the Greek meaning 'nose-horn'.

And in a similar vein...

Rhinos are endangered creatures because their horns are prized in various Eastern countries. This is true. What is a complete myth, however, is the Western belief that rhino horn is used as an aphrodisiac. Although the horn is prized in various types of medicine in China and other countries, notably as a cure for fever, it is not considered to have aphrodisiac qualities at all. In the conservation fight to save the rhinos, it's very important to get the facts right.

CHAPTER 3

Mythical menagerie

In which we reveal wyrd and fantastickal beestes of the worlde, and the reasons for their existence

The basilisk

It has been said that...

The basilisk is a winged creature with a serpentine body and a frilled neck whose gaze, if you meet it, causes instant death.

The truth

The belief that death came to unfortunates whose eyes met those of the basilisk makes it surprising that descriptions of the beast existed at all. Nonetheless, tales abounded of this creature, mainly from the deserts of north Africa. The name comes from the Greek *Basiliskos*, or little king (the Romans called it *Regulus* with the same meaning), and belief in its existence continued through into medieval bestiaries. Yet there was one way to deal with this fearsome monster: weasels, although not impervious to the basilisk's venomous glance, were able to cure themselves by eating the rue plant, and keep attacking the creature until it was dead. Pliny the Elder wrote: 'if a basilisk is thrown into a weasel's hole, the stench of the weasel will kill the basilisk, though the weasel will also die'.

In reality, the basilisk was probably no more than an exaggerated version of the Egyptian cobra, which can move along the ground with its hooded head raised. The snake's ability to spit deadly venom could easily make any distant observer of a clash between man and cobra believe that death had been caused by the gaze alone.

And what of the weasel? The Greeks and Romans who brought back tales of the basilisk would have heard about a small, carnivorous creature that is the main natural threat to the cobra. As the mongoose – whose quick movements and dogged determination for the kill helps it to take snakes down – is less well known in Europe, the weasel became a natural substitute.

And in a similar vein...

Cobras cannot be tamed by music: they don't even hear sounds in the same frequency band as humans. So the snakes that apparently sway to the sound of snake-charmers' gourd pipes are actually merely following the movement of those instruments.

Cerberus

It has been said that...

Cerberus is a many-headed dog that guards the entrance to the underworld.

The truth

On the basis that no living person has made the one-way journey in Charon's boat across the River Styx to Hades' underworld, and returned to tell the tale, then Cerberus, the mighty hound who bars the way to mortals who haven't paid the ferryman, can be assumed to be nothing but a Greek and Roman myth. Frankly, it's a pretty reasonable assumption to make. (Note: if you believe you have made and survived this journey, and feel a great temptation to contact the author of this book to regale him with your tales... please don't.)

Yet Cerberus (who is generally attributed with three heads, by some authors with 50, and by Horace with 100), is not the only mythological canine guardian of underworlds. Anubis was the original Egyptian god of the dead and embalming, who led souls on the path to their final resting place, while Garm, a mighty, slavering beast, barred the way to Helheim, the home of the dead in Norse mythology.

Why, then, was the dog so closely associated in ancient religions with such a terminal route? Wild dogs were common creatures in millennia past, the days of selective breeding and multi-tasking at the hands of man still some way off. They would often be found around loosely buried bodies, having scented precious meat just below the earth, and were frequent visitors to recent battle scenes. This gave them a link with the recently departed that eventually evolved into myth and legend.

And in a similar vein...

Cerberus, along with his equally terrifying siblings the Hydra, Medusa, the Nemean Lion and Chimera, was the offspring of Echidna, herself half-woman and half-serpent. The Australian echidna, also known as the spiny anteater, appears to have received its name from the ancient monster, but as 'echidna' meant 'poisonous serpent', how could this have come about? The answer appears to be that there was confusion in the naming: 'ekhina' is Greek for 'hedgehog', the animal the spiny anteater resembles most, and along the etymological route, the two words became blurred.

The dragon

It has been said that...

Dragons are fire-breathing, flying creatures with scales, horns and huge heads in which they keep precious jewels.

The truth

The dragon is perhaps the most enduring, widespread of mythological beliefs. While other beasties, from the griffin to the manticore, were steadily being laid to rest by science, the dragon persisted well into the eighteenth century, even the great taxonomist Linnaeus being called upon to identify some alleged remains of one (he denied their existence, however).

So how did they last so long, and why were they represented in so many countries? There is one, deep Jungian notion that the dragon is a collectively inherited expression of human fear, traceable back to the days when our ancestors lived in danger from snakes, big cats, raptors and fire, making the dragon, in effect, one huge, combined, genetically feared boogieman.

Well, that's possible and hard to disprove. But certainly, if such a latent fear existed, and evidence was found that a matching creature might once have lived, then the myth could easily have grown in stature. We're now in the world of prehistoric fossils, and there's one extinct animal whose giant skulls look just like those of the dragons of popular lore. The giraffokeryx, one of the several species of primitive giraffe, had a very large head with a long snout, and four great horns that swept back from its skull. Found in eastern Europe and Asia, these skulls could well have fuelled the draconian legend in the earliest times, and spread with man to other parts of the world.

And the precious jewels? Perhaps just the calcite crystals that can form on ancient skulls.

And in a similar vein...

There is of course one dragon walking the planet today, and that's the Komodo dragon of Indonesia. A huge reptile, growing up to 10 feet in length, it looks in reality nothing like the dragons of medieval tales, but had its name coined by one W Douglas Burden, who took an expedition to the islands in 1926 to bring one back for New York's zoo. Interestingly, his trip, upon which his wife came perilously close to death, inspired the 1933 film King Kong.

The griffin

It has been said that...

There exists an animal called the griffin, a flying creature with the body of a lion and the head of an eagle, that hoards great gold deposits in its nest.

The truth

Most mythological creatures each belong to the folk stories and legends of only a few ancient peoples, in only a few regions. Everyone invents their own bogeymen. Griffins, however, are different, tales of them coming through to us from many parts of the world, suggesting there may actually be some substance to the belief in their existence.

It appears there is. Most griffin legends originated in the great deserts of central Asia, and by the seventh century BC, had been relayed to the Ancient Greeks, who believed in them sufficiently to pass them on to the world. And why not? Buried near the surface of the sand of these shifting deserts still lie many fine skeletons of large lion-sized beasts, with huge beaks for mouths, and broad protuberances emerging from the backs of their heads that could easily be the basis of wings. Today, we don't call them griffins, we call them protoceratops, dinosaurs from the Cretaceous period, with bony frills on their heads, probably for courtship purposes.

The protoceratops – discovered by modern man in the Gobi desert in the 1920s – is one of the few fossils to be found at its own nest-site, a shallow indentation filled with about a dozen petrified eggs: stone eggs that to early civilisations may well have represented some sort of precious mineral, such as gold. The animal's strong hooked beak probably helped it eat the tough cycads and other prehistoric plants of 80 million years ago.

And in a similar vein...

Fascinatingly, there's a twist to this very story. Several protoceratops nests have been found with the skeleton of a small carnivorous dinosaur on top or nearby, suggesting that it was a predator of the herbivore's eggs. It was duly named oviraptor. In 1993, however, one of these eggs was found with an embryo inside – an oviraptor embryo! It's now believed that the nests belong to the oviraptor after all, and that, bird-like, it was sitting on them to incubate them. So why were the protoceratops so often nearby? There's so much still to discover...

The gulo

It has been said that...

There exists a creature called the gulo, in the lands of northern Europe, which exists only to feed, and is a cross between a lion and hyena, or perhaps a wolf and a dog.

The truth

Unknown to the ancients, because it lived in such northern European territories, the gulo was deemed to be a living morality lesson, thanks to its eating habits ('gulo' derives from the Latin for 'devourer').

To writers such as Olaus Magnus, the sixteenth-century Swedish geographer and devout Catholic, there were no baser habits than the Seven Deadly Sins, of which gluttony was a member. Of the gulo he wrote: 'Wherefore this Creature is the most voracious; for, when he finds a carcasse, he devours so much, that his body, by over-much meat, is stretched like a Drum, and finding a streight (narrow) passage between Trees, he presseth between them, that he may discharge his body by violence; and being thus emptied, he returns to the carcasse, and fills himself top full.'

The gulo does in fact exist, although it is neither a lion, a hyena, a wolf or a dog. It is a member of the weasel family, is known more familiarly known as the wolverine (*Gulo gulo*), and it mainly lives in the colder climes from Scandinavia to Siberia to Canada and the northern states of America. A ferocious three-footer, it has powerful jaws that enable it to rip even through frozen flesh, and will even tunnel through up to 10 feet of snow to reach living underground prey, such as marmots. It has to eat frequently to survive, but the belief that it disgorged its food to continue eating is false. The wolverine eats as much as it can, then drags any remaining parts of its meal back to its lair for later snacking.

And in a similar vein...

The wolverine, also known as the glutton, is associated with that particular sin, but only in the region in which it lived. In sixteenth-century Europe, in a determination to show that the animal kingdom exhibited habits above which mankind should rise, the pig was the creature most closely linked to gluttony, while the other sins were represented by the cow (lust), dog (envy), bear (anger), frog (greed), horse (pride) and goat (sloth, or sadness).

The lamb-tree

It has been said that...

There is a plant which, rather than growing flowers, grows lambs, which live their lives attached to its stalk.

The truth

In 1605, the botanist Claude Duret mentioned in his *Histoire Admirable de Plantes* an ancient plant that had apparently been referred to in ancient Hebrew texts. The plant, a native of India, was known as the Jeduah or Borametz.

'It was in form like a lamb,' wrote Duret, 'and from its navel, grew a stem or root by which this Zoophyte, or plant-animal, was fixed attached, like a gourd to the soil below the surface of the ground, and, according to the length of its stem or root, it devoured all the herbage which it was able to reach within the circle of its tether. The hunters who went in search of this creature were unable to capture, or remove it, until they had succeeded in cutting the stem by well-aimed arrows, or darts, when the animal immediately fell prostrate to the earth, and died.'

This 'lamb-tree', as it came to be known in the West, would also bestow upon any who ate its bones the gift of foresight.

All in all, quite a remarkable backstory for a plant that, today, we know simply as cotton. It's reasonably easy to see how the distantly viewed cotton fields of ancient Asia could be seen as miniature woolly creatures on fertile stalks, but for the extra edge that the story developed over the centuries, we have the fertile imagination of mankind to thank.

And in a similar vein...

Sir John Maundeville, a thirteenth-century knight whose tales of travel and adventure in the Holy Lands had for centuries been quoted as a sort of Crusaderly gospel, was only in the nineteenth century shown to be a fake, the imagined knight's exploits being a simple accumulation of hearsay and writings dating back to the time of Pliny. 'Sir John' was one of the alleged witnesses of the lamb-tree, but a further example of 'his' woolly thinking were the hen-sheep of China, which apparently bore white wool instead of feathers.

The mermaid

It has been said that...

The mermaid is a beautiful creature that sings so sweetly it lures sailors to their doom in treacherous waters.

The truth

Early in 1493, having discovered the New World, Christopher Columbus made a further discovery, one that suggested that he might have been at sea a little too long. 'On the previous day when the Admiral went to the Rio del Oro', records the ship's log, 'he saw three mermaids which rose well out of the sea... they came quite high out of the water, but were not as beautiful as they are painted, for somehow in the face they look like men.'

To be fair, Columbus wasn't the first to cast doubt on the famed beauty of mermaids. 'It has large nipples on its breast like a woman, long hands and heavy hair, and its neck and head are formed in every respect like those of a human being.'

recorded a Norwegian writer in 1250. '[It] is described as having a large and terrifying face, a sloping forehead and wide brows, a large mouth and wrinkled cheeks.'

These gorgeous creatures, we now know, are members of the sea-cow family, the manatees and dugongs. Found around many of the world's equatorial and southern tropical coastlines, these unusual mammals eat sea grass and vegetation only, and their expressive, mournful faces can often be seen coming up for air near fishing expeditions, then diving away again before reappearing further off, as if 'luring' sea-goers onwards. Their 'song' is actually a high-pitched chirp. There were five species left in the eighteenth century, now there are four. The Steller's sea-cow, the largest of them all, was hunted to extinction for its meat just 27 years after its discovery in the northern Pacific in 1741. The sea-cows' role in the legend of the mermaids is commemorated by their family name. Collectively, they are known as sirenians.

And in a similar vein...

When PT Barnum, the great nineteenth-century American showman, began exhibiting his mermaids at his outrageous freak shows, several members of the public were fooled. It's hard to see how, though, when you consider the creatures were simply stitched together body parts of fish, monkeys and baby orang-utans.

The su

It has been said that...

The su is a huge Patagonian beast that carries its young on its back.

The truth

A 'cruell, untameable, impatient, violent, ravening, and bloody beast,' wrote Edward Topsell of the su in his 1607 *Historie of Foure-Footed Beastes*. When a female, with its young on its back, comes under attack, she 'roareth, cryeth, howleth, brayeth, and uttereth such fearefull, noysome, and terrible clamor that the men which watch to kill her are not thereby a little amazed.'

It's hard to believe that Topsell, deploying his very best thesaurian writing style, is probably actually describing a sloth here. As sloths are associated with slowness, languor, indolence, sluggishness (sorry, slipped into Topsell-speak), it's hard to imagine them as impatient, untameable and violent. But then the Su is probably the mythical counterpart of the most amazing sloth of them all, the megatherium, or giant, sloth of Latin America.

Although the giant sloth, which was at least 18 feet long, is believed to have been extinct for around 8,000 years, it's quite possible that the still extant tales of the su derive from awareness of the creature inherited through the many generations by the people of those lands. (Some cryptozoologists, however, who study the science of unlikely and hidden creatures, believe that the mighty animal, that would have weighed as much as an elephant, survived until the modern era, perhaps until just a few hundred years ago, although this is unlikely.) And if, like modern sloths, it carried its young around with it, then a defensive mother would have been a most 'untameable' beast indeed.

And in a similar vein...

When is a sloth not a sloth? When it's a bear. When Western science came across a new creature in eighteenth-century India, they were convinced it was a bear-like sloth. Only once an individual had been shipped back to Europe in 1810, was it realised that the reason the animal seemed so like a bear, was because it was one. Today, the species reflects that early misunderstanding in its English name – sloth bear.

The unicorn

It has been said that...

The unicorn, a single-horned horse-like creature, is the most dangerous animal alive.

The truth

'The unicorn (monocerotem) is the fiercest animal, and it is said that it is impossible to capture one alive. It has the body of a horse, the head of a stag, the feet of an elephant, the tail of a boar, and a single black horn three feet long in the middle of its forehead. Its cry is a deep bellow.' Pliny the Elder, in his first-century AD tome *Natural History*, was one of many to believe in the fabulous unicorn. It seems hard today, however, to understand why a creature now viewed as the gentlest of animals, and a New Age symbol of purity and goodness, should once have been considered so violent.

The fact was, of course, that the unicorn never existed at all. Its origin probably lies in sightings of the Arabian oryx, an antelope with two straight horns which, when viewed side-on, only appears to have one (and in some cases, really does only have one, having lost the other in a territorial fight). Fleet of foot and powerful, it could well have appeared particularly ferocious, and certainly hard to capture.

The animal featured strongly in Christian allegory, too, representing in its single horn the unity of the Holy Trinity, and in its escapologist nature the determination of the soul to evade the fiery pits of Hell.

It was said, however, that there was one way to catch it. The Christ-like unicorn was said to have a particular devotion to virgins, reminding them of Christ's own mother's status, and would nestle up to them and lay their heads on their bosom, whereupon the hunter could slay them easily. It is unsurprising, then, that the beast has become a symbol of female vulnerability under threat from male-dominated aggression.

And in a similar vein...

The unicorn's horn was believed in the Middle Ages to have mystical powers: simply by being wafted over food or drink, it would reveal any hidden poison within by bleeding. Unicorn horn was therefore a precious commodity among noblemen during this era, giving rise to a huge trade in carved ivory fakes.

CHAPTER 4

Scientific slip-ups

In which we discover that we're not alone,
and even the experts can get it wrong

The badger

It has been said that...

The two legs on one side of a European badger's body are
shorter than the two on the other.

The truth

It was Edward Topsell who helped propagate the theory
in his widely consulted *Historie of Foure-footed Beastes*,
published in 1607. The book was published at a time when
scientific understanding of the world around us was lurching
forward – Galileo was developing new planetary theories,
alchemical experiments were giving way to more provable
sciences – but Topsell hadn't quite caught this mood. His
book is full of hearsay masquerading as fact, a sort of 'urban
myths of natural history' of its time. And most delightful it
is, too.

'Some say', he reported of the badger, that the legs are longer on the right than on the left, so that the creature 'runneth best when he getteth to the side of a hill'. As a consequence, the poor animal could more easily be caught when running across level ground, its lopsidedness causing it to stumble and fall.

It will come as very little surprise that, in fact, both forelegs on a European badger, or indeed any badger, are the same length as each other, as are both hindlegs. Topsell had merely picked up on an old myth based on the fact that badgers, whose setts are often built in undulating ground, can pick up quite a pace despite their short little legs, reaching speeds of up to 11mph. Shorter legs make for better running on slopes than humans can manage, leading to the quaintly human belief that if badgers can do it better than we can, there must be something odd about them – ie lopsided leg lengths.

And in a similar vein...

Like many nocturnal creatures, badgers were believed to be creatures of dark fortune, not just of dark nights. One eighteenth-century English folkloric rhyme took this to the extreme ('ullot', here, means owl):

Should one hear a badger call
And then an ullot cry,
Make thy peace with God, good soul
For thou shall shortly die.

The beaver

It has been said that...

Because beavers' testicles are of great value to human medicine, they bite them off to avoid capture.

The truth

In his magnificently titled *Physiomedical Dispensatory* of 1869, William Cook described castoreum as 'a hard substance found under the prepuce of the penis on the beaver – castor fiber. There are two of these on each animal, and they resemble two testicles. They have a strong and unpleasant animal odour, which is impaired by age; and yield their properties to rectified spirits.' Cook was mentioning the substance, which is in fact an oily secretion from two plum-sized abdominal glands on a beaver, because it had been used since Roman times to cure constipation and impotence.

Although these scent glands are not actually the beaver's testicles, the similarity of their name – castoreum – to the word 'castrate' ushered in an intriguing confusion. By the Middle Ages, some European naturalists had decided that beavers, in attempt to render themselves useless to mankind, would bite off their scent glands, and eventually this transmogrified into the idea that they would completely castrate themselves. Some even suggested that beavers would defend themselves by biting off a hunter's testicles. One way or another, medieval beavers were having a ball.

Castoreum still turns up in some homoeopathic medicine cabinets as a cure for epilepsy, and is also used in perfumery, but the fervour for digesting beaver scent gland juice rather fell out of fashion by the nineteenth century. A new oil was found, however, from the shrub *Ricinus*, and as it replaced castoreum as a purgative medicine, manufacturers decided to give it a similar name: castor oil had been born.

And in a similar vein...
Contrary to most cartoon depictions, beavers do not use their tails as mortars to help them pack logs together with mud to make their dams. The flat broad tails are used as rudders to help them swim, and slapped against the water as an alarm signal when danger approaches.

The bird
of paradise

It has been said that...

Birds of paradise spend all their time in the air, never coming
to rest, and so they have no need for feet.

The truth

There are over 40 species of the remarkable and ostentatious
birds of paradise, most of which live in New Guinea in the
Pacific. Their plumes boast almost every colour of the rainbow,
and they use them in courtship displays that dwarf for
technicolour grandeur those of just about every other creature.
Yet, despite the fact that a major part of those displays involves
dancing and prancing to impress females, for centuries many
believed that these spectacular birds had no feet.

The distinguished nineteenth-century naturalist, Alfred Russel Wallace, relates the story: 'From an unknown antiquity the natives of New Guinea have been accustomed to preserve the skins of these beautiful birds, and barter them with the Malay traders, by whom they are universally known as "burong mati," or dead birds, because they had never seen them alive. As the natives used always to cut off the feet in order to preserve them more easily, the Malay and Chinese traders concluded that they had none; and all sorts of stories were told about their living continually on the wing, and being in fact birds of heaven, whence originated the names of "birds of paradise" and "birds of the sun" given them by the early Portuguese and Dutch writers.'

In the 1750s, when Linnaeus was composing his massive taxonomic listing of the world's creatures, he perpetuated the myth, although probably with tongue in cheek. He named the family *Apodidae* – Greek for 'footless'.

And in a similar vein...

Some people believe that the bird of paradise plants of southern Africa, the Strelitzia family, are so named because they are fed upon by the avian birds of paradise, but as these live on a completely different continent, this is not the case. They are named because their magnificent orange and blue flowers vaguely resemble the birds.

Birds of the world

It has been said that...

There are about 8,600 species of bird in the world and, as many of them are endangered, this number is likely to fall.

The truth

In 1951, the naturalists Ernst Mayr and Dean Amadon came up with a figure for the global number of bird species. By their calculations, there were 8,590, and for the generation who grew up during the birdwatching boom of the 1960s and 1970s, this was the definitive figure. As the years rolled by, and worrying population counts of individual species began to fuel conservation concerns, many ornithologists began to predict that the total would fall below 8,000, and possibly even further.

Then, in 1990, Charles Sibley and Burt Monroe released a new figure. They'd done their sums, and by their reckoning, there were now 9,672 species – a full thousand and more up on the count four decades previously. How could this be?

Welcome to the world of lumpers and splitters. Many of the world's species of animal have colonies, or entire groups, that vary in form, habitat or behaviour from the main group. Lumpers tend to class them as subspecies of the main animal, while splitters prefer to give them individual specific status. By the 1990s, when Sibley and Monroe were calculating their list, the splitting community was holding sway, and most of the birds now seen as species in their own right were previously viewed as 'mere' subspecies back in the 1950s.

And, of course, each time a subspecies is 'split' away from its original species, it takes its population count with it, resulting in two smaller populations where once there was a single larger one. More species, more to worry about.

And in a similar vein...

Surely it's impossible to discover a new species the size of an elephant? In 2001, some scientists decided they had done just that. DNA fingerprinting suggested that the African elephant was really two separate species, one of the savannah, and one of the forest. So have we discovered a new species of elephant? The debate continues.

The brontosaurus

It has been said that...

The brontosaurus was a huge vegetarian dinosaur with a long neck and tail.

The truth

During the 'dinosaur wars' of the late nineteenth century, when fossil hunters were competing across America to be the first to find and name new creatures, occasional lapses in professional rigour slipped through the net. In 1877, one such hunter, OC Marsh, discovered some bones of a specimen of a mighty vegetarian dinosaur, and revealed it to science as the apatosaurus. Two years later, he discovered a similar skeleton that was lacking a head. Fuelled by hope that he had found something new, he searched until he found a skull four miles away that he thought must belong to the same species. He named the creature brontosaurus – 'thunder lizard'.

Unfortunately for Marsh, the skeleton he had found was indeed that of an apatosaurus, and the skull belonged to another species altogether, a camarasaurus. By the time the rash mistake was revealed, in 1903, the name brontosaurus had stuck, even though there was no such animal.

Was Marsh simply over-zealous in his hopes of finding new creatures? Or was he deliberately cheating in order to boost his reputation? Perhaps the answer lies in his earlier discovery. Ironically, apatosaurus, the animal that for a while doubled up as a brontosaurus, translates as 'deceptive lizard'.

And in a similar vein...

Huge sauropods like the apatosaurus were once believed to have been water-dwelling dinosaurs, their body weight requiring the buoyancy of lakes in order to keep it up. In fact, no sauropod bones have ever been found in such areas, and their feet would have been unsuitable for wading through mud anyway. Some palaeontologists now think that the apatosaurus, far from being weak, may even have been able to stand on its hind legs to reach vegetation.

The coelacanth

It has been said that...

The coelacanth was a prehistoric fish that died out with
the dinosaurs.

The truth

Today, the coelacanth is probably as well known for having
'come back' from the dead as the dodo is for having not. But
it was only a few decades ago that this six-foot, multi-finned
fish of the Indian Ocean was believed to have ended its 350-
million-year lifespan with the great extinction of the dinosaurs
65 million years ago.

It was a couple of days before Christmas 1938, when
Marjorie Courtenay-Latimer, a museum curator in East
London, South Africa, wandered down to the dock to wish
the local fishermen a merry Christmas. The trawler *Nerine* had
just pulled in, and its captain, Hendrik Goosen, made a habit
of keeping any unusual – and inedible – catches for Marjorie's

tiny museum. On that night, he had a strange type of rock cod, but little else, and Marjorie offered her greetings and turned to go. She noticed the 'rock cod's' fin sticking out from the pile of rays and sharks on deck, and pushing them aside, saw 'the most beautiful fish I had ever seen'.

It was the scientific world's rediscovery of the coelacanth, a fish that was not to resurface again for another 14 years, the second specimen appearing off the Comoro islands in 1952. Today, it is believed there could be a population of something up to 1,000 of the fish, in various deep-water cave colonies of the ocean.

And like the fish itself, its rediscoverer enjoyed a long, long life. Marjorie Courtenay-Latimer lived on at East London until 2004, dying at the age of 97.

And in a similar vein...

For many years after its discovery, it was believed that the coelacanth had been living in underwater Comoro caves for all those hidden 65 million years. Yet the Comoros are only a few million years old themselves, suggesting that the mighty fish may have lived along various parts of the ancient Gondwanaland coastline, before that great land mass steadily split up between 160 and 50 million years ago. As a result, there could be coelacanths living in many parts of the Indian Ocean.

The dromaeosaur

It has been said that...

Members of the prehistoric raptor family have a huge claw on each of their feet that they use to slash their prey.

The truth

Anyone who saw Spielberg's *Jurassic Park* will be very aware of the sickle-shaped claw of the raptor. The chilling way in which it tapped its murderous weapon on the kitchen floor as it stalked two terrified children was one of the film's most memorable moments. Yet recent, and certainly post-Spielbergian, research now suggests that the claw, rather than being used for slashing as previously supposed, was actually a gripping tool.

A team of scientists, hired to replicate the action of a dromaeosaur, the real-world creature that is closest to the cinematic raptors, discovered that the claw wasn't quite as tough as once assumed. In a robotic reconstruction utilising steel, aluminium, hydraulics, carbon fibre and Kevlar®, they forged an action that mimicked as closely as possible that of the original dinosaur, in terms of both movement and strength. It was able to cut through lighter animal substances, such as chamois leather, but the team found it was incapable of slicing tougher skins, such as that of a crocodile. As this latter is probably the closest we have to dinosaur hide, then the claw would have been useless as a cutting tool. As one of the scientific team stated upon announcing their results in 2005, 'using the claw to slash would have been like me trying to disembowel you with a plastic spoon'.

It's more likely, then, that the raptor family used their outlandish tools to grip their prey, having first pounced, then torn their flesh away with their teeth. It also shows just how rapidly palaeontological research is developing.

And in a similar vein...

When Spielberg unveiled the initial plans of his mighty dinosaur film, many experts scoffed. Raptors, they said, only grew to about half the size – about six or seven feet – that Spielberg was planning to show them at. Then, in October 1991, the utahraptor was discovered. It stood at up to 20 feet tall! The news was released shortly before the film, and Spielberg had the kind of natural PR that money simply can't buy.

The hedgehog

It has been said that...

European hedgehogs steal apples by rolling across them as they lie on the ground, thus collecting them on their spikes. Then they make their way back to their apple-filled nests and munch happily on their stolen fruit through the winter.

The truth

The Roman Pliny the Elder (23-79AD) was fascinated by the natural world, and his *Naturalis Historia*, a mighty collection of 37 tomes, was the first major attempt to chronicle the natural world as it was understood in its day. Many of these observations still hold up today, but some of them are just romantic nonsense. Witness the hedgehogs: the belief came about because apples were sometimes found lying on the ground with small holes in them, and hedgehogs were sometimes seen chomping away on them. Two and two were put together, and four was not the answer found. Hedgehogs do not carry apples on their backs, and the narrow holes are likely to be caused by insect larvae. Nonetheless, later writers took the myth on to even greater heights, suggesting that hedgehogs actually climbed trees to shake the apples off, and even, in the case of the seventh-century writer Isidore of Seville, claiming that they sliced bunches of grapes off vines with their spikes, then skewered them, too.

The apple myth has endured over the centuries, and still makes a good tale. In 2004, the Spanish children's author Javier Saez Castan published *The Three Hedgehogs*, for three- to seven-year-olds, in which the tiny little trio collect apples on their spikes much to the chagrin of the local farmer. She sets out to kill them the following spring, but a heavily laden apple tree has now grown on the site of their midnight feasts, bearing apples aplenty for the whole village. The three zeroes have become heroes, and the moral is clearly revealed: scrumping, that ancient art of apple-stealing, bears dividends.

And in a similar vein...
Ancient Egyptians revered the hedgehog as a symbol of reincarnation, believing it to die in the autumn and come back to life in the spring. All the while, of course, it was merely hibernating.

The hippo

It has been said that...

The closest living relative to the hippopotamus is the pig.

The truth

Classifying the stocky hippo, with its massive head and chunky legs, has always been a problem. The ancient Greeks lumped it together with the horse (the word 'hippopotamus' means 'river horse'), but modern science had for 200 years placed the creature alongside the pig family, mainly because of the shape of its molars. Yet there were some dissenters to this theory, and in 2005 they announced the final proof they'd been looking for. The hippo's closest cousin is in fact... the whale.

Blood proteins and molecule structures had already laid the foundation for this new theory, but it was fossil records that clinched it. Recent discoveries have shown that water-loving ancestors of the cetaceans (whales and dolphins) split into another branch about 50-60 million years ago called the anthracotheres. While the cetaceans abandoned land altogether, the anthracotheres remained land-based, and spread out across the continents over a 40-million-year period, eventually almost dying out during the Ice Age. Today's hippos are their only survivors.

Of course, this raises the suggestion of a further intriguing relationship. Hippos are members of the artiodactyla group – mammals with cloven hooves – and this new evidence now means that the whales, which it now appears diverged away from the ungulates, could well be placed in this enormous group, too, alongside cows, sheep... and those old friends the pigs and horses!

And in a similar vein...

For centuries, mankind thought that hippos sweated blood. But why? The mistake was fairly understandable: the huge creature does indeed secrete a reddish substance, not blood, but a mixture of two pigments that provide it with an effective sunscreen during the hot African days.

The iguanodon

It has been said that...

Iguanodons were early forms of giant reptile, and had the
ability to walk upright on their hind legs.

The truth

Perhaps because it was the first dinosaur to be discovered by
modern science, the iguanodon has been surrounded by more
than its fair share of erroneous theories.

It was first discovered by Mary Ann Mantell while out for
a stroll around the English village of Cuckfield, Sussex in
1822. Noticing an unusual fossil lying by the side of the road
among some rocks, she pocketed it and passed it on to her
husband. Gideon Mantell was a doctor and a fossil collector,
and he quickly identified the item as a fossilised tooth of
some unknown creature. Deciding that the tooth was like a
giant version of the iguana's, he named the creature that it
must have come from 'iguanodon' – 'iguana tooth'. As other
similar creatures began to appear in rocks around the world,

the initial view was that they were early reptiles. They were classified as dinosaurs – 'terrible lizards' – although we now class them in a group separated from the reptiles.

Back with the iguanodon a new theory was developing. A series of bird-like footprints belonging to the dinosaur was discovered on the Isle of Wight, leading Thomas Huxley, a proponent of the theory that dinosaurs evolved from birds, to announce in the 1860s that iguanodon must have been bipedal. The reconstruction of the dinosaur's skeleton at London's Natural History Museum accordingly placed it in a two-legged upright position. This stance remained until the 1990s, when studies of the creature's vertebraic structure revealed that a fully grown iguanodon must have been four-footed after all in order to carry its weight.

So the iguanodon was not a reptile and probably did not walk on two legs, although it still may be a relative of early bird life. It is, without doubt, however, a perfect example of the still evolving understanding of prehistoric life on Earth.

And in a similar vein...

During the mid-eighteenth century, full skeletons of the iguanodon began to appear, including among them a sharp horn, some inches long, that early palaeontologists placed on the animal's snout, like a rhinoceros. It was some decades before science realised that the horn was in fact a thumb spike, used either for defence or garnering food.

The leopard

It has been said that...

Leopards are the offspring of lions and panthers.

The truth

Pay attention, now, this one is going to take some following.
Originally 'panther' was the term given to virtually any large
feline that wasn't a lion or a tiger. Today, in North America,
pumas are still sometimes called panthers, while the jaguars of
South America are also occasionally given the epithet. The most
famous panthers are the black, or melanistic, forms of leopards
and jaguars that live in India, Africa and South America.

With 'panther' in such generic use, the animal we now call
the leopard needed its own name, and for this naturalists
turned to an ancient term for panther that had been used
since heraldic days, the 'pard'. But there was another animal

wandering around that was closer to the size of a lion, yet carried the spots of a pard. Early naturalists decided it must be a cross between the two animals, and called it a leopard – 'leo' plus 'pard'. Eventually, it was realised that this animal, which we now call a cheetah, was not a hybrid at all, but the new term 'leopard' had gained such common usage that it remained in the language, and came to mean the animal previously called the 'pard'.

So here we are today with leopards, wandering around with a name that suggests they are a cross between lions and themselves. The actual name for such an offspring is the 'leopon', and these hybrids have in the past been created in private zoological collections. Crosses between lions and tigers are called ligers or tigons (depending on which species was the father and which the mother), while jaguleps and jaglions are crosses between jaguars and leopards or lions.

And that's that. Simple, isn't it?

And in a similar vein...

The pard, the heraldic term for panther, was often depicted as being multicoloured, and was said to give off a sweet smell. This latter belief may have derived from the 'violet glands', not of big cats, but of their fellow carnivores, foxes and wolves, which give off a strong smell, although not a particularly sweet one.

The mosquito

It has been said that...

Malaria, the illness that claims at least a million lives each year, is caused by infected air, particularly around swampy areas, and is nothing to do with animals.

The truth

It is remarkable that the origins of malaria, one of the most destructive conditions known to man, should have remained hidden for so long, but it was only towards the end of the nineteenth century that the connections with mosquitoes were first made. In the 1880s, the Frenchman Alphonse Laveran isolated the parasites that caused malaria in patients' bloodstreams (for which he later won a Nobel prize), and in 1897, the Briton Ronald Ross showed that these parasites were transmitted by mosquitoes.

Until this point malaria, which was probably even in existence in prehistoric times, had long been a misunderstood bane of human life. For centuries, no one seemed to know where it came from, and in the eighteenth century, the Italian Lancisi, noting that it was common in the marshy lands around Rome, decided that the swampy gases in the area must be creating a poisonous air, or miasma. This gave the illness its name – malaria is simply Italian for 'bad air'.

So much for Western science. Some 2,500 years ago in India, the medics Charaka and Sushrutha had written a series of texts which still form the basis of Ayurvedic ('science of health and long life') medicine today. Writing some 100 years apart from each other, they explained the disease in great detail, showing great familiarity with its symptoms and effects. They also noted that its origin suggested a possible connection with... mosquitoes.

And in a similar vein...

Many people think that all mosquitoes suck your blood, but in fact it's only the females. They need the protein from the blood they collect to help them develop their eggs. Just to add insult to injury, recent research has shown that having sucked up your blood, they almost immediately expel their waste materials on your skin, too, to reduce their weight for take-off. Well, thank you very much.

The nightjar

It has been said that...

The nightjar, that enigmatic European summer visiting bird
that hunts by night, steals milk from sleeping goats.

The truth

There's nothing like being nocturnal for ensuring that the human
race treats you with great suspicion, and the nightjar is no
exception. This cuckoo-shaped visitor from distant Africa arrives
in small numbers in Britain each year, where it proceeds to hide
by day among the heathlands of the South, its barred, streaked,
mottled plumage providing it with magnificent camouflage on
branches while it sleeps. But by night, it becomes a mysterious
hunting force, its huge gape expanding to hoover up insects as it
flies, its silent flight interrupted only by the occasional clapping
together of its wings; its cricket-like churring echoing as it
perches high on a tree trying to attract a mate.

Such a cryptic bird was bound to attract legends born of superstitious minds, but it ended up with quite an odd one. It was believed that at the dead of night, the bird would steal silently up to a field of sleeping goats and, opening its huge mouth, suckle at them until it had drained them of milk. So strong was this belief that the scientific name of the nightjar family is *Caprimulgidae*, 'goat-milkers'.

The belief, which can be traced back as far as Aristotelian times, came about because nightjars are dependent upon insects for their food, and can therefore often be seen flying around livestock where insects congregate at night. As goats were one of the main domesticated animals of the ancient Greeks, and as they were often lactating during the time when the nightjars arrived from their migration, the conclusion that the two were connected was all too easily made.

And in a similar vein...

The whippoorwill is an American cousin of the nightjar, and it was once believed in some of the southern states that the number of times a bachelor heard the bird's distinctive 'whip-poor-will' call would equal the number of years before he would finally get married. As the bird is fairly vocal, it's a wonder anyone got married down there at all.

The parrot

It has been said that...

If you throw a parrot at a rock, instead of flying away, it will use its beak to absorb the impact.

The truth

This rather curious belief, which was recorded in medieval bestiaries, rather begs the question: how did they know? Did medieval scholars spend their time throwing parrots around in quarries to see what would happen? Sadly, the bestiary does not specify the research, but the likely source of the theory is the bird's habit of apparently bashing its beak against hard objects such as tree branches for no apparent reason.

Of course, there is a reason. Parrots' beaks are formed with keratin, the same substance that is the foundation of our fingernails, and consequently they keep on growing. To avoid having two mandibles that cross over each other, or even that grow into each other, the bird has to grind them down constantly.

There's no doubt that a parrot's bill is a formidable tool – as anyone who has ever been nipped by one will testify – but as to whether a parrot could absorb the impact of a blow against a rock, it's highly unlikely.

Even more unlikely is it to survive the further advice provided in one of those natural histories, the Aberdeen Bestiary: 'Its skull is so thick, that if ever you have to admonish it with blows to learn – for it tries hard to speak like men – you should beat it with an iron rod. For when it is young, up to two years of age, it learns what it is told very quickly and keeps it firmly in mind; when it is a little older, it is forgetful and is difficult to teach.'

And in a similar vein...
To 'parrot' is to repeat someone else's words
without recognition or intelligence. Parrots,
however, are very intelligent birds, able to
identify objects by size and shape, and count at
least up to six. They also exhibit signs of play,
another mark of intelligence.

The pelican

It has been said that...

The pelican kills its young in the nest, then pierces its own breast to revive them with its blood.

The truth

There is a passage in Psalms that to the modern eye makes little sense. Psalm 102, being a prayer of the afflicted who calls out for help from Yahweh, includes the sentence: 'I am like a pelican of the wilderness, I have become as an owl of the waste places, I watch, and have become like a sparrow that is alone on the housetop'. The owl with nothing to look at and the sparrow alone without its flock, both make sense... but a lost pelican? Why that particular bird?

The pelican was once held in esteem as an icon of immaculate parenthood, sacrificing itself to bring life to its offspring. The symbolism came about from the belief that the bird, in response to the greedy demands of its young, kills them then wounds itself so that its blood can bring them back to life again. In reality, pelicans feed their young by tipping their heads forward and regurgitating their food, the contents of which will have become red in colour. To the distant observer, it may indeed look as if the bird has pierced itself (the huge pouch under its beak looking like flapping skin).

Unsurprisingly, in time the bird became a symbol of Christian sacrifice, Thomas Aquinas writing: 'O Loving Pelican, O Jesu Lord, Unclean am I but cleanse me in Thy blood'. Even Shakespeare was aware of the allusion, having Laertes say in *Hamlet*: 'To his good friends thus wide I'll open my arms; And like the kind life-rendering pelican, Repast them with my blood'.

And in a similar vein...

The Egyptians similarly viewed the pelican – or Henet – as a protective parent, placing symbols of it alongside the dead in their tombs, believing that their loved ones could emerge from the birds' cavernous beaks into the next world. Intriguingly, they also believed that pelicans would protect the bodies from snakes, presumably from having seen the birds store long wriggly sea creatures in their pouches.

The platypus

It has been said that...

There is no such thing as the duck-billed platypus, and specimens that have been presented to science are no more than an elaborate hoax.

The truth

When the Governor of Australia was first presented with the body of a platypus in 1798, he couldn't work out exactly what he was looking at. So he did what any sensible yet perplexed governor would do under the circumstances, and sent it on to the British Museum in London for identification.

There, the eminent scientists were most displeased. After all, they were busy folk, and didn't appreciate having to deal with such an obvious hoax as a mole's body fitted up with webbed feet and a duck's bill. 'Must be the work of Chinese taxidermists,' said one. 'Maybe God intended Australia to be a prison camp for monstrous animals, too,' mocked another.

When they read the accompanying note that the creature laid eggs, too, they simply scoffed and turned on their heels. (Why were the Chinese blamed, incidentally? For years they'd been mocking up fake mermaids with monkey bodies and fish tails.)

But the platypus was no hoax. It took four years of poking and prodding until the London scientists decided that the animal had been stitched together by nature, rather than the Chinese, and for the next century, argument raged about under which category of animal it should be classed. Even Darwin puzzled over it, exclaiming that 'surely two distinct Creators must have been at work'.

Today, we class the platypus (Greek for 'flat foot') as a monotreme, along with the echidna, the only egg-laying mammals in the world. But did it evolve from the same clade of the evolutionary tree as the marsupials, or are the monotremes the evolutionary descendants of another type of mammal altogether? The scientific world researches on…

And in a similar vein…

For many years it was thought that the platypus slapped its tail against the water to warn others of impending danger, rather as a beaver does. In fact, the creature dives quickly under the water when threatened, using its tail to thrust itself downwards, and making a splash into the bargain.

The robin

It has been said that...

The European robin and the common redstart are but one
bird. They change into each other depending on the season.

The truth

Aristotle's *History of Animals* is a collection of observations
on the wildlife of Greece and surrounding countries, and
his conclusions drawn, written around 350BC. Sometimes
the great philosopher draws very fine conclusions – as when
noticing the apparent friendliness of dolphins, he decides them
to be social creatures – but occasionally he slips up. He notes
correctly that several birds change their plumage from season
to season, but on one particular occasion he takes an extra,
slippery step.

'The erithacus (or redbreast) and the so-called redstart change into one another; the former is a winter bird, the latter a summer one, and the difference between them is practically limited to the colouration of their plumage.'

In Britain, it's hard to see how the mistake could be made. Redstarts are indeed summer visitors, returning to spend their winters in Africa, but the little robin is with us all year round.

In Aristotle's Greece, however, the robin was much less frequently seen during the hotter months, being more of a northern European bird, and migrating down to the Med and North Africa during the winter. As they were rarely seen together, Aristotle was able to use them to advance his theory of bird transmutation, a theory which also erroneously conjoined the wintering blackcap and the summer-visiting garden warbler.

And in a similar vein...

How did the robin get its red breast in the first place? According to Christian legend, this once brown bird, noticing a man hanging on a cross and wearing a crown of thorns, tried to ease his pain by pulling out one of the largest of those thorns. A drop of Christ's blood landed on its breast, staining it with goodness evermore.

The salamander

It has been said that...

The salamander is so cold that it lives unharmed within fires, and can extinguish the hottest flames.

The truth

Salamanders are moist-skinned amphibians found in many countries mainly in the northern hemisphere. The substance that some species such as the fire salamander secrete, once believed to put out flames, is a toxin called salamandrin that can burn the mouths and eyes of small mammals that might consider the creature a tasty treat. But as the salamander prefers damp areas, how did the legend arise that it can live within fires?

It's all to do with hibernation. Like many amphibians, the salamander seeks out piles of dead wood to hide out in for the winter. As often as not, those piles are actually collections of logs for use as firewood. Once the blaze begins, the salamander emerges scampering from the flames, its bright blue and yellow mottled skin making it stand out from other small fleeing creatures. And as the wood that it has chosen is likely to have been damp, there's a reasonable chance that the fire will soon go out, giving rise to its legend as an extinguisher.

The belief persisted well into the Middle Ages, and was often used by Christian scholars in their texts on the underworld. Augustine of Hippo, the fifth century theologian whose writings greatly influenced church doctrine, wrote: 'if the salamander lives in fire, as naturalists have recorded, this is a sufficiently convincing example that everything which burns is not consumed, as the souls in hell are not'. It was fortunate that he added the 'if'.

And in a similar vein...

'Hush puppies', fried corn doughballs used as a side dish in the American South, probably get their name from being used by al fresco diners to feed their dogs and keep them quiet. But another unlikely theory has also been put forward: at times of great hardship salamanders, known in the area as 'mud puppies', were once fried in corn meal as an unpleasant, but desperate dish. No one liked to admit they'd been driven to such dire straits, however, hence the hush that surrounded the meal.

Swallows and martins

It has been said that...

European swallows and martins hibernate during the winter.

The truth

Swallows are among the more charismatic of Europe's summer
avian visitors from Africa, and with their hirundine relatives
the martins, tend to stay on a bit later than most other species,
so conjecture about where they might go during the winter
was always likely to be stronger than with other birds.

Aristotle was one of many to state that swallows hibernated
in trees, a belief that persisted up until the sixteenth century.
By the seventeenth century, however, the French ornithologist
Pierre Belan had run a series of fairly conclusive tests on
various bird species, keeping them in captivity during the
winter months in reasonably natural conditions, and watching

for signs of hibernation. He found none, and backed by his and other evidence, the theory of migration was becoming much stronger than that of hibernation.

Yet, bizarrely, there were still many who wanted to believe that swallows and martins in particular did not depart European shores. Some observers, even into the eighteenth century, were hanging on to the theory, even claiming that they'd raised sleeping swallows from the mud at the foot of riverbeds. The fact that swallows and martins are often seen on late summer evenings hawking for insects just above the water's surface probably helped give credence to this theory.

Even Gilbert White, the great British naturalist of Selborne in Hampshire, got caught up in the great hirundine debate, writing in 1781 of his monitoring of house martin movements, and concluding that 'so far from withdrawing into warmer climes, it would appear that they never depart three hundred yards from the village'.

And in a similar vein...
Having concluded that no birds hibernate,
ornithology was stunned in 1948 to discover
that the common poorwill, a nightjar-like bird of
western North America, is able to put itself into
a deep torpor during the winter months, a state
approaching hibernation. Whether or not it actually
hibernates fully has yet to be determined.

The swan

It has been said that...

Shortly before they die, swans burst into melodious singing, anticipating their end. This gives rise to the concept of the swan song, a grand final act.

The truth

According to Plato, while sitting in his cell awaiting his execution, Socrates said: 'Will you not allow that I have as much of the spirit of prophecy in me as the swans? For they, when they perceive that they must die, having sung all their life long, do then sing more lustily than ever, rejoicing in the thought that they are about to go away to the god whose ministers they are. But men, because they are themselves afraid of death, slanderously affirm of the swans that they sing a lament at the last, not considering that no bird sings when cold, or hungry, or in pain, not even the nightingale, nor the swallow, nor yet the hoopoe.'

Although views differed as to the function of the swan song – it was either a lament for the coming end or a welcoming for the glory to come – the fact was that the main premise was wrong. Wild swans, such as whooper and Bewick's in Europe, or trumpeter in America, are very vocal birds, and very social, too. In fact, they use their noisy trumpeting, 'whooping' and bugling as a means of keeping the family group together. Should a swan be in danger, it and others will call vociferously, an extraordinary sound comprising a variety of notes that could sound vaguely like a song. Their graceful shape and movement help compound the myth.

The mute swan, meanwhile, isn't. It gains its name from its comparative silence when contrasted with wild swans, but it is in fact capable of various hisses and grunts.

And in a similar vein...
Perhaps because of its black face, the mute swan was believed in the Middle Ages to have black skin, and for a period became a symbol of hypocrisy – white of outside appearance, dark of soul within.

The tenrec

It has been said that...

The tenrec is the world's rarest mammal.

The truth

Anyone who as a child could be found eagerly poring over
the animal pages of the *Guinness Book of Records* would be
familiar with the tenrec. They could probably tell you that
it has its place in the book thanks to a single specimen of its
species found in 1928, and that the specimen appeared to be an
intermediate form between the two families of hedgehog tenrecs
and shrew-like tenrecs. Had they investigated further, they
would now be able to tell you that it was found in Madagascar,
that it is insectivorous, and that it was named in honour of
a former president of the Madagascan Academy, one Dr

Fontoynont. They would be able to point out that it has spines on its back and flanks, but none on its head or underparts.

If you meet such a person, hand them a copy of the *Guinness Book of Records* published after 1987, and ask them to find the tenrec now. They won't be able to, for the simple reason that the animal does not exist. Comparative anatomic research in that year showed that the single creature titled simply 'tenrec' was in fact an immature version of the already known greater hedgehog tenrec.

The real world's rarest mammal? The title tends to swing from one creature to another depending on population flow, but in 2006 the *Guinness Book of Records* had the rarest land mammals as the Javan rhinoceros, with 60 individuals left.

And in a similar vein...

Tenrecs were once considered just to have filled the ecological niche on Madagascar of hedgehogs and shrews, some species resembling the former, some the latter, but today we know of about 30 species of them, and they do all sorts of things. There are mole-like tenrecs, that burrow underground, and there are jumping tenrecs that have mouse-like tails. There's even a water tenrec with webbed feet and a keeled tail. Tenrecs are one of the most diversely evolved mammal families in the world.

INDEX

ABOUT THINK BOOKS

THINK
BOOKS

Think Books publishes books to suit a variety
of interests, from popular entertainment to the
environment, walking, gardening and more.

To find out more, please visit www.think-books.com